How To Say 'I Do'

Allen & Unwin
83 Alexander Street
Crows Nest NSW 2065
Australia
Phone   (61 2) 8425 0100
Fax   (61 2) 9906 2218
Email: info@allenandunwin.com
Web: www.allenandunwin.com

National Library of Australia
Cataloguing-in-Publication entry:

Newman, Mandy.
How to say 'I do'.

Includes index.
ISBN 1 74114 433 7.

1. Marriage service - Australia. 2. Weddings - Australia.
I. Newman, June. II. Title.

395.220994

Set in 11/13 pt Minion by Midland Typesetters, Maryborough, Victoria
Printed by Griffin Press, South Australia

10 9 8 7 6 5 4 3 2 1

How To Say 'I Do'

Planning your perfect civil marriage ceremony

Mandy Newman with June Newman

ALLEN&UNWIN

To my husband—MN

To Alan—JN

FOREWORD

I first got married in the 60s when I was twenty years old. All I could think about was my gorgeous shantung silk dress that hugged all my curves (they were in all the right places then—SIGH), my lovely pointy silk shoes which are now fashionable again, my bouffant hair crowned with a tiara and elaborate veil and my darling new husband.

I didn't give a thought to the marriage ceremony. That was the priest's job and it was a given that the service would be held in a church and I would be told what to say.

Over a decade later my dear husband died, and I had a second go at a wedding in the 70s. Again it was a church service that was solely orchestrated and conducted by the priest with no thoughts, ideas or directions from me. (If you're curious, we divorced three years later—never marry on the rebound of a great loss.)

Oh how differently I would do it all now.

Since starting the first ground-breaking postgraduate course ever to be offered in Australia for civil celebrants at the University of Victoria (now at Monash University), I began a journey of discovery about the importance and meaning of ceremony and ritual in our lives, and the need to share and include people in our communities in this experience.

Marriage is one of life's major passages; it is one of the most profound rites of passage that a person or couple can experience. Through the act of a marriage ceremony we leave behind the single life to start a new reality. A marriage ceremony is a space in which to make that transition—by making a public commitment in front of your family and friends for life. This is an incredibly powerful moment that demands a structure that reflects who you are, where you have come from, what your love means to you both, and also reflects your dreams and desires for your future.

And so I am now an authorised civil marriage celebrant and I have found that the most commonly asked question from couples is: 'What do I have to do? I do not know where to start'. All I could give them was a cobbled collection of photocopies and book references as I couldn't point them to one book which I felt reflected what I thought a marriage ceremony should be all about.

After waiting for a number of years for someone else to write the book that I was looking for, I decided that I should have a go myself. So here it is. It's what I think, what my daughter thinks, plus lots of ideas, suggestions and experiences from other celebrants.

Thank god for the many wonderful contributions that have so generously been supplied by my fellow Monash colleagues and many others—it has always been my belief that no, one person has all the answers. Their contributions have added a depth that otherwise would not have been possible. My great dream is that this book will guide and inspire couples to have a go at creating the marriage ceremony of their dreams. There are so many gifted celebrants who are skilled and trained to help you weave your colours into your own individual tapestry that will celebrate your love and dreams for your future.

A closing thought: make the marriage ceremony the centre of the celebration, it and you deserve it. Have a fabulous marriage.

June Newman

CONTENTS

ACKNOWLEDGMENTS

To Professor Fred Klarberg's dream. To all the celebrants we interviewed and who so generously contributed material: Pat Lane, Norman Knipe, Geoffrey Baird, Judy Seregin, Judy Peiris, Jocelyn Fausset, Marita Wilcox, Nitza Lowenstein, Peter Hyland, Clive Rumney, Cherie Scott, Myly Nguyen, Catherine Bearsley, Andy Seymour.

To Michael Brown from Brown's Family Lawyers in Sydney, Donna Dohi from New Zealand Dream Weddings, Robert Colosimo-Young from the Department of Internal Affairs in New Zealand and Tracy Floro from NSW Registry of Births, Deaths and Marriages.

Jo Paul for taking a punt on us and for being such a source of calm and enthusiasm and for hosing down any inclination we had to panic. Jeanmarie Morosin and Susin Chow for finding a decent book in the material we gave them. We are in awe of your attention to detail!

All the couples that we interviewed.

Father Brian Johnstone, Roland Fishman, to all the gang at afr.com; Natalie Oliver, Charlotte Sims and Sharon Aris for making all this possible.

Mandy: To Harry and Ruby—Mummy is out of the office now. To Mum for being Mum.

June: To Mandy for being stoic, effervescent, char . . . oh shut it Mum!

Mandy: The biggest thanks of all goes to my lovely Andrew Duncan. Everyday I congratulate myself for marrying you. You make everything possible. What would I do without you?

June: To Alan, who was the eternal optimist and believed in my eagle that now has soared.

Mandy and June Newman

INTRODUCTION

I never thought that I would get married. I didn't believe in it. Or so I thought. When Mum enrolled in the first university-run course in civil celebrancy in Australia in 1996 and she and I began to talk about what she was learning, I started to change my mind. Marriage wasn't just about the passing of a woman from father to husband, it was something much deeper—a tradition that had been a part of human civilisation for thousands of years. What I didn't realise is that marriage is a rite of passage that celebrates love and the decision of two people to try and build a life together. It publicly ritualises the transition from the state of a single person to that of being part of a couple, ideally for life. The act of marriage therefore is deeply significant.

Around this time, I attended a wedding ceremony between two friends and I was amazed at how heartfelt and moving the declarations of love were from the groom—a man I would have typified as an emotional brick. Further, you could almost feel the love in the room. Mushy I know, but real. What could be wrong with that?

So I did a major backflip and much to my boyfriend's surprise, in 2000 I said, 'Let's get married!' As we are not particularly religious, we thought that we would have a civil ceremony so I tried to find a book about it and guess what? There was nothing out there that spoke to me. There were mountains of bridal magazines and herbal-flavoured texts big on mush and meringue but light on cool and classy.

At the same time, Mum had graduated from her course and was marrying couples all over Melbourne who were all chanting the same thing, 'We want a civil ceremony. Where do we start? There is nothing out there.'

So we decided to combine our talents and write a book together, the kind of book we would like to read or refer people to. It only took five years for the idea to come to fruition!

And so here it is, bursting with ideas and inspiration. There is no other book like it. Between these pages you will find examples of Shamanic and medieval weddings, the wedding vows that Thorne and Macy from 'The Bold and the Beautiful' made to each other, song suggestions such as Jet's *Are you gonna be my girl*, and a send-off with a touch of the navy. One of the strengths of this book is that it includes material from many celebrants (including Mum) to show you how different ceremonies can be.

It is practical and fun and its message is please, please, please, do what you want. There are so many possibilities. Take the time to find the right celebrant for you. There is someone out there who will be able to give you what you want.

Then go and create the wedding ceremony of your dreams so that when you and your lovely wake in each other's arms the morning after your wedding, you can say to each other, 'I feel married, that was terrific and I would not change a thing.'

Isn't that the best way to start your journey as husband and wife?

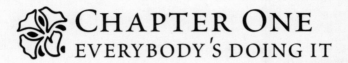

CHAPTER ONE
EVERYBODY'S DOING IT

It's time to stop panicking. You've done the right thing. You've bought this book. This is the roadmap for your civil marriage ceremony. If it makes you feel better—you are not alone. Church marriages are on the way out and civil marriage ceremonies are in. In Australia in 2002, 55 per cent of marriages were performed by civil celebrants (ABS 2004). These sorts of figures are echoed throughout the world.

Why civil?

It seems that most of us go civil simply because we are not religious or we feel that traditional religious services are too stiff and formal.

Christine didn't want a religious wedding. She says, 'I was born and raised a Catholic but I don't follow it. I'd been to a lot of weddings in churches and they just seemed too impersonal. I didn't want to have to swear in front of God and all that jazz.'

For Fiona and Anton, a civil service was a solution to a dilemma. Fiona says, 'We had two different backgrounds. I was Catholic and he was Greek Orthodox and we didn't want a ceremony that favoured one or the other. So we decided to have a civil ceremony that would be about the both of us as much as possible.'

And for Lisa and John, a civil service seemed to offer them the opportunity to have the kind of ceremony they wanted. 'We're not churchgoers and it seemed a bit hypocritical to have a church ceremony,' says Lisa. 'And we wanted to have something quite relaxed, outdoors and that reflected our lifestyle.' Also, because John had been previously married in a church, Lisa was very conscious of not doing the same thing. She says, 'It was a fresh beginning with no echoes of the past.'

Be prepared

Once you mention the C word—Civil marriage ceremony—be prepared. Some people won't flinch but other responses will range from 'But what do you do in a civil ceremony?' to 'You can count me out!' When Gaby married civilly, she encountered a lot of flak, 'Everyone I met, everywhere I went, people were treating me strangely because I wasn't doing the traditional wedding thing . . . it was like we weren't really getting married.'

However, as more of us marry civilly, these ceremonies will become more familiar. When Julia and James married in a civil ceremony, Julia was surprised that many of the older guests said the wedding was 'most unusual' but the best they had ever been to. Sombre out. Fun in.

Is a civil service the same as a 'real' service?

Yes. Of course it is. A civil ceremony is legally recognised as a marriage. In many countries in Europe, only civil marriages are legal.

What do you do at a civil marriage service?

Keep reading and find out!

CHAPTER TWO
LEGAL MUMBO JUMBO

Getting married is one of the biggest life changes that you may ever undergo. It involves legally changing your status from that of a single person to that of married. This chapter explains some of the formal aspects of marriage, from the legal hoops you have to jump through to get the rings on your fingers, to how your responsibilities change once you sign your name on a marriage certificate.

Let's first look at the legal requirements you have to fulfil to have a civil marriage ceremony in Australia and New Zealand.

What must a civil wedding contain in Australia?

Australian law defines marriage as 'the union of a man and a woman to the exclusion of all others, voluntarily entered into for life' (*Marriage Act 1961*). Scary huh!!!

The law says that:

- If you wish to marry, you and your partner must be at least 18 years old. A person aged 16 or 17 years who wishes to marry must obtain parental consent and an Order from a Judge or Magistrate allowing the marriage.

- Your marriage may take place on any day, at any time and at any place in Australia, or within Australian territorial waters or airspace.
- At least two people over the age of 18 years must be present at the marriage ceremony and act as witnesses.
- You, your partner and your registered celebrant must sign the Notice of Intended Marriage form, and provide it to your celebrant at least one calendar month and a day before the wedding date and not more than eighteen months before your wedding date.
- A birth certificate must be provided if either you or your partner was born in Australia. If either of you was born overseas and a birth certificate is impossible to obtain, your celebrant will advise you of what will be required.
- If you or your partner has been married before, evidence of how it ended will be needed—either a Decree Absolute in the case of divorce, or if the previous partner has died, a death certificate.
- You and your partner must sign a declaration saying you believe that there is no legal impediment to your marriage.
- You and your partner must be given a brochure called *Happily Ever . . . Before and After* (*Marriage Act 1961*, Form 14A) which contains important information for people planning to marry. The celebrant must also inform you of the range of pre-marriage counselling services available to you.
- During the ceremony the registered celebrant must say to the parties, in the presence of the witnesses, the words, 'I am duly authorised by law to solemnise marriages, according to law. Before you . . . are joined in marriage in my presence and in the presence of these witnesses, I am to remind you of the solemn and binding nature of the relationship into which you are now about to enter. Marriage, according to law in Australia, is the union of a man and a woman, to the exclusion of all others, voluntarily entered into for life', or words to that effect.
- The ceremony must take place in the presence of a registered marriage celebrant.
- Both parties, the two witnesses and the celebrant must all sign each of the three marriage certificates.

- During the ceremony each party must say, 'I call upon the persons here present to witness that I . . . take you . . . to be my lawful wedded husband/wife' or words to that effect.

What must a civil wedding contain in New Zealand?

Interestingly, the *Marriage Act of New Zealand 1955* doesn't actually define marriage as having to be between a man and a woman. But, in a case that went to the New Zealand Court of Appeal in 1988, the court held that the Marriage Act applies to marriage between a man and woman only (NZ Ministry of Justice, 1999). The law in New Zealand says that if you wish to marry, you must first organise a registered marriage celebrant and agree on a time and place for the marriage to take place (NZ Department of Internal Affairs, 2004). A registered marriage celebrant may be a Registrar of Births, Deaths and Marriages (NZ), a civil marriage celebrant, a minister of a church or a person connected with an approved organisation.

Both of you:

- Must be 16 years of age or older, although parental consent is required if either party is under 20 years of age.
- Must be free of impediments to marry. If you have been married previously, that marriage must have been dissolved by a court of law.

Either you or your partner must then:

- Go to a Registrar of Births, Deaths and Marriages office to complete a Notice of Intended Marriage form and sign a statutory declaration saying you are legally free to marry.
- Pay for your marriage licence.
- Wait three days for your marriage licence to be approved. It is valid for three months.

At your marriage ceremony:

- At least two people over the age of 18 years must be present at the marriage ceremony to act as witnesses.

- The ceremony must take place in the presence of an authorised marriage celebrant.
- During the ceremony each party must say, 'I . . . take you . . . as my husband/wife' or words to that effect.
- The celebrant must pronounce the couple to be husband and wife.
- Both parties, the two witnesses and the celebrant must all sign two copies of the marriage certificate.

Who can be a witness?

In Australia and New Zealand, anyone—as long as they are over 18 years of age.

Do witnesses have to be the same sex as the bride and groom?

No, in both Australia and New Zealand.

I can't find my birth certificate, will my passport do?

No. If you were born in Australia you must use your birth certificate. If you were not born in Australia you must provide proof of birth.

   You don't need a birth certificate to apply for a marriage licence in New Zealand.

Can I use a photocopy of my birth certificate?

No. In Australia, only official extracts from the appropriate Registry of Births, Deaths and Marriages will do.

Does it cost anything to apply to marry?

In Australia, no (unlike the rest of the process). At least not directly. The cost is absorbed in the celebrant's fee.

In New Zealand, depending on where you choose to marry, between NZ$120–170.

What name do I sign my marriage documents in?

In Australia, before you are married, you must use the name on your birth certificate, unless you have changed your name by deed poll. If this is your second (or third) marriage, you must use the name by which you are known and have the supporting documentation.

Can someone other than an authorised marriage celebrant lead a civil marriage ceremony?

In both Australia and New Zealand, people other than authorised celebrants can play a role in a civil marriage ceremony. However, there are strict guidelines that must be observed (Nance 2004). There must be a registered celebrant in attendance who:

- consents to be present at the ceremony as the responsible registered marriage celebrant
- takes a public role in the ceremony
- identifies themselves to the assembled parties, witnesses and guests as the celebrant registered to solemnise the marriage
- is responsible for ensuring that the marriage ceremony is carried out according to law
- recites the Monitum (not applicable in New Zealand)
- will remain in close proximity to the ceremonial group to hear and see the vows exchanged
- will intervene if necessary
- signs all the official documentation.

Auckland celebrant Jocelyn Fausett has been asked to stand in at a number of Wiccan weddings. At a recent celebration, *Carmina Burana* was playing in the background, guests stood in a sacred circle, a practitioner read the rites and Jocelyn completed all the legal aspects of the ceremony. 'I'm quite tall and I've got silver hair and I have to say that I have been mistaken for the chief Wiccan,' she says.

Can a priest/rabbi/reverend marry me in a civil service?

It all depends. There are many religious clergy who are also civil celebrants. Sounds impossible but it's true. Vikram and Ella, for example,
were married by a Hindu priest who was also a civil celebrant.
Celebrant Norman Knipe from Upper Hutt in New Zealand, is a
Congregationalist minister as well as a civil celebrant and has performed many civil marriage ceremonies with religious elements. He
became a celebrant when he realised that some people were missing
out on the type of wedding service that they wanted. 'I didn't think
they should miss out,' says Norman.

What if I want to get married overseas?

The lure of an exotic location or the chance to get away from over-
enthusiastic family members means that marrying overseas can be an
attractive proposition. If this seems like a great idea, get on the phone
and start calling consulates or embassies of the countries where you
would like to marry. Some countries have quite strict requirements.
For example, if you wish to marry in France, either you or your
betrothed have to reside in the town in which you wish to marry for
at least 40 days preceding the marriage (http://www.nolo.com). In
some states in the US, you have to undergo a blood test, to check both
partners for venereal diseases or rubella, yet in Las Vegas, there is no
waiting period and the marriage licence bureau is open 24 hours a day
on Friday and Saturday (as Britney Spears demonstrated).

Make sure you fulfil all the legal requirements of the country
you are marrying in, plus any requirements from your country of
origin. Many countries need a document stating that you are legally
able to marry, typically called a Certificate of No Impediment. In
Australia, this form can be obtained from the Department of
Foreign Affairs and Trade's website, and in New Zealand from the
Department of Internal Affair's website.

If you use Google and enter 'overseas marriage Australia' or
'overseas marriage New Zealand', you will be directed to the overseas
marriage section of the appropriate government department.

Make sure you have copies of your marriage certificate before you
return home. Marriages that occur in a foreign country are generally
legally recognised but cannot be registered in Australia or New Zealand.

Make sure you dot all the i's and cross all the t's . . .

When Jerry Hall filed for divorce from Mick Jagger, he claimed that they had not fulfilled all the Indonesian legal requirements when they married on a beach in Bali, so Jerry could not make a claim on his estate as his wife (The *Irish Examiner* 19 January 1999). (They eventually resolved the matter.)

Commitment ceremony

Some of us may want to make a lifetime commitment to another person but for whatever reason do not wish to, or cannot, marry. In this case, you can have a commitment ceremony. This type of ceremony can have all the elements of a marriage ceremony but none of the legally binding aspects. Many same-sex couples choose this option.

Liz and Mark

When Liz and Mark started thinking about making a formal commitment to each other, Mark in particular was uncomfortable with the idea of getting married. 'Marriage was never a strong thing in my family,' he says. 'I didn't want the state or the church to certify my relationship. But I recognise the importance of commitment. Your relationship is the most important thing in your life. So I wanted to separate the issues of certifying the relationship and the importance of commitment.'

He also recognised that ceremony is important in people's lives. 'I wanted to have a ceremony but I didn't want to have anyone charged with making official entries into the government record.'

So Liz and Mark devised a commitment ceremony that basically mirrored a marriage ceremony. It included askings, vows, readings and songs and was officiated by a loved and respected older friend of the couple but was not sanctioned by the state. Both Mark and Liz were very happy with the ceremony.

In New South Wales, as the legal status of defacto couples is not the same as that of married couples, Liz and Mark, in consultation with a lawyer, developed and signed a cohabitation agreement. 'We thought that it was important that we understand what we had committed to. It clarifies what our responsibilities are and it was a way of making us think of what we were committing to,' says Mark.

While they were both delighted with their ceremony, over time, Liz has had a slight change of heart. 'I think that now I would have preferred to have been married because it is difficult to explain to other people—they tend to believe that you are either married or you're not. Sometimes I actually say that I'm married but then I always feel like I'm lying.'

What about marriages between same-sex couples?

In Australia and New Zealand, the marriage law is very clear. Marriage is defined as being between a man and a woman. Therefore marriages between same-sex couples are not legally recognised— yet. But the times, they are a changing. In 2003, various cities in Canada and the United States started to recognise unions between same-sex couples.

In June 2004, the New Zealand parliament began discussing the Civil Union Bill which, if passed, will give equal recognition to marriages and gay or straight civil unions (Tunnah 2004). While in 2004 in Australia the Tasmanian *Relationships Act* came into force. For the first time in Australia, same-sex couples can officially register their unions at the Tasmanian Registry of Births, Deaths and Marriages (Darby 2004).

While not yet registered as a marriage celebrant in New Zealand, Sue Neal has been conducting commitment/marriage ceremonies for gay couples on the North Island for the past three years. She and her partner, Glenda, married in 2004. Together for ten years, they chose a traditional wedding ceremony with a hand-fasting ritual.

'Needless to say it was a lovely ceremony in which my sons, their father, Glenda's sister and mother all took an active part in the ceremony and the readings and blessings,' says Sue. After the ceremony they shared a sumptuous feast and danced the night away. 'It was so lovely,' remembers Sue, 'because it was such a joyous occasion and everyone there wished us well and enjoyed the occasion for what it was—a celebration of our love.'

So carry on anyway! Marriage is for all (even if the law doesn't recognise it).

Pre-marriage education

In Australia, when you have an interview with a civil celebrant and inform them of your intention to marry, they are legally obliged to hand you a '*Happily Ever . . . Before and After*' brochure; otherwise known as Form 14A. This is a small pamphlet which outlines marriage education programs available to you and lists the ways in which your legal obligations change once you marry. Celebrants are also supposed to inform you about pre-marriage education programs and give you points of contact for pre-marriage education services.

Now, most couples think, 'We don't need to do a pre-marriage course, we love each other!' Well, that's all fine and good, but how far does love get you when you have two kids, an ageing mother and a partner who is working their guts out to pay the mortgage yet you feel like your life is passing you by?

Pre-marriage education is not about how much you love someone—it's about working out whether or not you are going to go the hard yards and be able to make a life together. It picks up your strengths and 'growth' areas—as they say in the field.

Pre-marriage education covers a range of topics such as lifestyle, friends and interests, personality match, communication, problem-solving, religion and values, parenting issues, extended family issues, sex, finance, and marriage. It's not a compatibility test like you do in a magazine but a tool for teasing out the issues that make marriage a constant work in progress. As Don Burnard, a psychologist from the Family Relationships Institute in Melbourne with more than 30 years' experience in delivering relationship development courses for couples, says, 'It's not just marriage that we need to prepare for. It's parenting. It's middle age and retirement.'

Some of the specifics marriage education looks at are: How do you deal with disagreements? Do you both want the same things for the future? Who is going to do the washing up and the cooking? How are you going to balance careers with children or plans to travel? Do you have similar ideas about how children should be raised?

How much sex is enough? (OK, that question may not come up directly but it may be discussed indirectly.) How do you handle money? Do you think marriage is for life? How do you argue? Fairly?

Looking at that list, my husband and I should have done the test—and Mum and her second husband (now divorced) should have done it too! And that is the point. The more we discuss the things that break us up before they escalate, the better chance we have for marrying someone and creating a life with someone we love and who wants the same kind of life.

How do I find out about pre-marriage education?

In Australia, your celebrant should provide you with a list of educational providers. Religious and secular organisations run courses with different focuses and emphases, so do your homework before committing to a course. Courses are generally one day and three to four sessions in length. Other points of contact are Relationships Australia, the Marriage and Relationship Educators' Association of Australia, Relationship Services Whakawhanaungatanga in New Zealand and other counselling services.

The Australian Federal Government has an interesting website www.relate.gov.au where you will find useful information on relationships, family, love and life. The Department of Family and Community Services also produces a fantastic booklet entitled 'Two equals one' which covers all sorts of topics that couples should discuss before sliding rings on their fingers. It includes some very interesting questionnaires on how you communicate with your partner, for example, does your mind drift off when your partner is talking to you? YES. The answers may not be pretty but they could spark discussions that could make your marriage that much better.

Changing your name

You don't have to change your surname when you marry. But many women do. The 2003 *Bride to Be* magazine's 'Cost of Love Survey' revealed that 86 per cent of readers surveyed would take their husband's surname. In Australia and New Zealand, you don't need to send in any forms to your local registry of marriages if you want to take your husband's name. However, if you wish, you can apply to formally change your name with the registry.

Be warned though—in Australia, you cannot use the Certificate of Marriage issued by the marriage celebrant on the day of the marriage to have personal documentation, such as your driver's licence and passport, changed to your married surname. You will require a Standard Marriage Certificate which you also sign on the day of your marriage. It is the copy with the declaration on the back and a registration number. You will need to request a copy of it from your celebrant or apply for an official copy from the Registry of Births, Deaths and Marriages if you wish to change your driver's licence and so on.

In New Zealand, you do not have to formally apply for a name change. When you marry, you sign two copies of a marriage certificate. The bride and groom take one copy on the day and it is the celebrant's responsibility to send the other to the Registrar of Births, Deaths and Marriages within ten days of the ceremony being performed. The couple may then receive a registered copy. Either of these certificates is proof of name change, should you require it.

When you change your name, you may have to change your driver's licence, passport, car registration, bank accounts, insurance, credit cards, superannuation, tax records, electoral enrolment, memberships and more. There are websites that sell 'changing your name kits' so you can do it all in one go.

Problems with keeping your name

It's surprising but it's true. I never thought for a moment to change my name, much to the sadness of my mother-in-law. I married in my mid-30s and it just seemed crazy to take my husband's surname. However, once I had a child, I entered into a whole quagmire. It took almost a year for our doctor to file my daughter's documents next to mine—their computer couldn't cope with my surname being different from hers. An early childhood nurse assumed that I had broken up with my husband when I first met her and I had to explain that my surname was different from my daughter's. And don't even try to explain different surnames to tradespeople and so on.

Some people choose to take a new name

Sydney writer, Tegan Bennett, told the *Sydney Morning Herald* that when she married her husband, Russell, they became the Daylights. It began as a kind of nickname for the couple, she says:

> When we were first together six or seven years ago, we were sitting around with another close friend, talking about how cool it would be if when you got married you both took a new name so you could share the same name as your children. And somehow Daylight came up and all three of us have at some time claimed it was our idea. So, we used to jokingly call each other Mr and Mrs Daylight, and then it became our email address, and then people just started calling us The Daylights. And when we got engaged my mother made us a quilt and stitched each of our names into it, and below them, 'Tegan and Russell Daylight'. When the time came, double-barrelling was no option because Russell's name was already hyphenated. And by then, we were so established as the Daylights that it was the only name in contention (Wood 2002).

How your legal status and responsibilities change when you get married

Who gets what

Once you're married, if you die without a will in Australia, your spouse will inherit all or some of your property (Commonwealth of Australia 2001). If you have a will, you will need to examine it closely for it to apply after your marriage. Talk to your spouse, buy a will kit or talk to a solicitor to make or adjust your will, particularly if this is your second marriage and you have children. It's not something that we like to talk about, but you may have to, if you want to ensure financial security for your children.

For Australians, the brochure *Happily Ever . . . Before and After* explains in detail how your responsibilities change.

In New Zealand, any will made before your marriage is

automatically revoked and you will need a new will, unless the will has been made with the impending marriage in mind (New Zealand Law Society 2003). For more information, contact the New Zealand Law Society.

The legal differences between married couples and defactos

It's interesting that in New South Wales, Australia, marriage comes with additional legal entitlements from those of defacto couples. For example, if you come to divorce and you are married, the Family Court will look at the contribution that each of you has made and your future needs, which means that if you had any children their future needs are protected. However, if you are defacto and you have children and you separate, the 'courts only look at contribution, they don't look at future needs. There is no adjustment for children. That can be a difference of anywhere between 10–25 per cent in terms of the split up,' says Michael Brown, a family law specialist. Crikey!

Michael remembers that when he started as a lawyer, a barrister said to him, 'Silly women enter defacto relationships.' He was right! As Michael points out, 'It's generally the woman who is not making the financial contributions and it's generally the woman who is left with the children at the end and she's not going to get any adjustment for that.'

What's interesting is that this is not the case in the state of Queensland in Australia, or in New Zealand (New Zealand Law Society 2002). Defactos and married couples share the same legal rights with regard to property settlement. Who would have thought there would ever be a legal incentive to marry? However, some discriminatory provisions still exist between defacto and married couples in New Zealand. A defacto partner has fewer rights in coroner's hearings and is banned from being buried in the same cemetery plot! These laws are all set to be standarised by the Civil Unions Bill which was presented in the New Zealand parliament in June 2004 (Tunnah 2004).

If you're keen to know more, check out the law in your state or territory.

CHAPTER THREE
LET'S START AT THE
VERY BEGINNING

The first step for planning your wedding ceremony is actually quite simple. You and your partner need to chat about what you would like to do in your ceremony and what kind of ceremony you want. The major hurdle that most people encounter, at this stage, is themselves. We feel the fear and as Henry Miller said, 'Every day we slaughter our finest impulses' (Miller 1987). And why not? It's bloody scary. What if we look stupid? What if everybody cringes when I explain how I love him? What if? What if? What if?

For example, with my wedding, the major roadblock was me. I was terrified of pledging that I would love my husband for the rest of my life. At the time of our marriage, I wasn't able to plan ahead for six months. Thinking about it challenged every deep-seated fear I had. I had tried to avoid loving and committing to someone all my life and now I was going to get married? Oh pl-eease. So when it came to planning our vows, we had a most interesting discussion, which left my husband amazed, about how—'I wasn't prepared to say that I would be with him forever but I was most willing to try!'

I was also unconfident about realising the Rat-pack-come-bossanova-type service and reception I dearly wanted but never really articulated. I was concerned that I wouldn't pull it off and it would look ridiculous. And what about expressing our love for each other—would everyone cringe?

Now I am pleased to report that not everyone has as much baggage as me. But some of these issues can get in the way when you're planning a marriage ceremony. And we shouldn't let them. No, we're not all disciples of 'Oprah', able to spill our feelings for all and sundry. Nor are we all poets laureate able to wax lyrical about how we love thee. But we all love. And we can love well. And we should celebrate it.

In our crazy, mixed-up world where, in the name of modernity, we've demolished so much of the infrastructure that reminds us of why it is great to be alive, a marriage ceremony is a celebration of life and hope—a window, a day where we proclaim that we believe in life and the future. You may only marry once in your life, so make the most of it.

Now is the time to banish all those fears and insecurities. Never has it been more important for your confidence to rise to the top. You will never experience a day that goes as fast in your life. It will be over in a blink, so make the most of it! Please. Please. Please. Feel your fears but do whatever it is your heart is pleading with you to do. Your wedding day is the day for dreams to live and for you to declare who you are and how you love each other.

Melbourne celebrant Judy Peiris has observed that:

> People who are witnessing the wedding really appreciate the personal part. They love it. It makes them get in touch with the ceremony. You see people start to cry because of the emotion. And the only way you get emotion is if you connect the ceremony with the couple. If you don't then you are just reading out words.

Sasha and Dave had the courage to say what they truly felt when they made their vows. What Dave said to Sasha so moved Dave's father that, when he got up to make his speech at the reception, he said, 'I've been to lots of weddings, and some of them have been mine [he's been married three times] and I've never cried at a wedding and this is the first time because of Dave's vows.' (Awww—tissues please!) And that is what weddings are all about—declarations of love.

Remember, you are not alone in this process. Consult Chapter 5 of this book for lots of ideas and inspiration. Also, when you find the right celebrant, they will help weave your dreams and desires into a beautiful ceremony. But the celebrant needs material to start the process and you and your lovely are the only ones who can provide it.

Some of us know what we want . . .

Vanessa and Richard wanted a simple marriage service. They didn't want any readings and they didn't want to dramatically change their wedding vows. Vanessa says, 'You love each other and you are agreeing to formalise it and go forwards forever. End of story. It's not about us showing everyone how much we love each other because we just do. It's about everyone coming together for a drink and a party.'

Gaby and Marcus also wanted their wedding ceremony to be a 'communal celebration of what was already in place.' Gaby says, 'It wasn't a new thing. We'd been together a long time, we'd been living together. Accepting to get married, to me, was the wedding. So the ceremony was all about family and friends and the main thing was we wanted them all involved.'

They chose readings that were long enough to give all the people they wanted to include in the ceremony a chance to participate, and they wrote their own vows and devised a unity candle ceremony. 'We weren't just going to take a package ceremony. It had to be something that we really could attach ourselves to, because this is our life,' says Gaby.

For the rest of us . . .

It's time to start thinking about what kind of ceremony you want. What do you want to say? How do you want to say it? What, if any, kind of symbolic actions do you want to take? Open a bottle of wine, sit down with your partner, take a confidence pill, don't judge yourself nor think about the end point, and answer the following questions. These are the sorts of questions that a good civil celebrant would ask. However, if you don't have a clue how to answer some of them, don't worry—by the end of this book you will (and then come back and have a good look at them again)! Armed with this information, you will have taken the first step to creating your ceremony.

Getting to know you

- How and where did you first meet?
- Did the sparks fly or was it a slow burn?
- How long have you been together?
- Why don't you want to 'just' live together anymore? What's changed?
- What is the worst disaster that you've made it through as a couple?
- What's the best time that you've ever had together?
- What do you love doing more than anything?

Ceremony

If you have been to any other wedding ceremonies, what did you like about them? What didn't you like?

- Why do you want a public ceremony, instead of just going to a registry office?
- Will there be anyone else participating in your ceremony, and how will they be involved?
- What dreams do you have about your wedding?
- Do you want a theme for your wedding?
- Will you have music? Live or recorded? What is your all-time favourite song? Do you have a song that is your song—as a couple?
- Do you have any favourite readings that you would like to include in your marriage ceremony?
- Do you wish to incorporate elements of your religion or cultural background into the ceremony?
- If you've been married before, do you have any regrets about the ceremony from your previous marriage?

Setting

- When do you want the ceremony to take place? Do you have a favourite season, or time of day?

- Where would you like to get married? By the sea? In a park? At your local club? On a cliff face? Deep in a forest? On a yacht? In a hot air balloon?
- What kind of atmosphere do you want? A medieval village setting, for example, or a beach theme? What do you have to do to create it?
- Will you have an altar where the vows are exchanged?
- How will the guests be gathered? And who will tell them what to do?
- How will the bridal party enter and exit?

Symbolic acts and rituals

In addition to talking, how are you going to show how you feel about each other and the commitment you are undertaking?

- Would you like to incorporate the use of bells, breaking of bread, drinking of wine or lighting candles into your ceremony?
- Would you like to have a handfasting ceremony? Or would you like to jump over a broom together?
- Would you like to release doves, butterflies or bubbles at the conclusion of your ceremony?

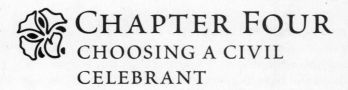# Chapter Four
CHOOSING A CIVIL CELEBRANT

The civil celebrant is the backbone of your ceremony. As one civil celebrant said so succinctly, 'Your day hinges on the celebrant . . . and your ceremony could be shit if you don't have the right one.'

When Ella and Vikram were looking for a civil celebrant, Vikram realised, 'You don't want someone who can just help you fill out the forms, you want something quite different.' And you do. Marriage is a significant ritual—a rite of passage. You may only do it once (or twice) in your life, so you want someone who is up to the task.

What qualifications does a celebrant need?

All civil celebrants in Australia are registered by the Registrar of Marriage Celebrants, who is an officer of the Commonwealth Attorney-General's department. You can check if the celebrant you are interested in is registered by going to the marriage celebrant's section of the department's website. Some civil celebrants may have completed tertiary studies or a TAFE course in celebrancy. In

Australia, all registered civil celebrants are now required to complete annual professional development classes.

In New Zealand, a celebrant may be a Registrar of Marriage, a civil marriage celebrant, a minister of a church or a person connected with an approved organisation. Some celebrants would have completed studies in celebrancy.

What should you look for?

There are all types of civil celebrants. The most important thing is that you choose someone you feel comfortable with, who is going to take your wedding seriously and who's clear that it is your wedding not theirs. Sasha and Dave found that 'While the others went through what information they could give us and how to pay, June said, "I'm just here to guide, it's your day—make it special." It was such a simple thing but we walked away and said "that is really what it's about" and so we went with her.'

In addition to making you feel comfortable, a celebrant also needs to be a source of information and ideas—an expert in the art of marriage. You need a creative soul, someone who is open-minded, and who has a good knowledge of ritual and how rituals work.

Celebrants also need to command attention—not in the sense of being General Scary Pants but rather they need to be able to focus proceedings and create a sense of occasion. Melbourne celebrant Geoffrey Baird advises couples to look for someone who can 'address a crowd with liveliness rather than sounding like they are reading the phone book.'

You need someone who is aware of stage management. They should ask you sensible questions, such as, if you're having an outdoor wedding, is there a readily available power supply for musicians?, and where will the sun be?

And although it's not essential, if you have access to your celebrant via email, your ability to consult and develop your ceremony is that much greater.

Finally, your celebrant needs to be available—not just on the big day, but throughout the period leading up to your wedding. Find out how many weddings they are officiating at on your nominated day. Will they be too busy? Remember, brides are generally late, so what will you do if your celebrant is delayed?

Where can I find a civil celebrant?

Ask your friends

Once you start the wedding marathon, it's amazing how many people you know who have just been married. Ask your friends or work colleagues if they know of a good celebrant.

Search the Net

Increasingly, most civil celebrants advertise their services on the Internet. The Net is the easiest way to find someone. You can contact associations of civil celebrants, such as the Australian Federation of Civil Celebrants and the Celebrant's Association of New Zealand, though not all celebrants belong to these organisations. All the large wedding websites have lists of celebrants as well. Log onto Google and search for civil celebrants in the region where you live and you will be presented with many choices.

Or look through the local paper or phone directory—old-fashioned but a good source for a local contact.

Call them

If you like the sound of their voice and are happy with what they have told you, make an appointment to see them.

Meet them

Go to their house, or arrange to meet at a café and see if you gel with them. Remember, they are providing you with a service, so if you don't like them, find someone else! That's what Lisa and John wish they had done. Lisa says they didn't get off to a very good start with their celebrant. 'We got caught in traffic going to her house, but when John rang her on his mobile, she ticked him off for being late, saying, "Well that's just not on." And when we got there, she had cats draped everywhere. John hadn't brought his decree for dissolution of his first marriage and she said, "Well I can't proceed without that!" But even though we got off to a really bad start, we felt duty bound to use her because a friend had recommended her.'

Lisa had ideas of John and his friends surfing out to sea after the ceremony and of using a surfboard to symbolise their union but, because she felt so uncomfortable after her first meeting with their celebrant, she just made her choices from the narrow set provided by the celebrant. 'I felt really inhibited by her and because she made it quite clear that she was displeased with us, I felt like we were on the back foot, almost apologetic, and said, "Oh well, that will do."'

Shop around

If necessary, interview at least three candidates, to ensure you find someone who is right for you both. There are some fantastic celebrants out there, but you may need to dig around to find the right one for you.

When Vanessa and Richard were looking for a celebrant, they were very clear about what they didn't want. 'We didn't want a woman,' says Vanessa. 'At weddings that we had been to, the women celebrants had always been in really strange clothes and stood out in all the photos.'

Richard says, 'We went to one wedding and the celebrant was dressed like a magician's assistant. She had a midnight blue satin dress on with a Chinese collar and half moons and stars on it, and a split up to the hip. She kept leaning in to get into the photos and putting her knee forward so the split would open!'

'So we decided that a woman was too risky,' Vanessa says. 'At least with a man, he would blend into the background, in a dark suit.'

Vanessa and Richard weren't happy with the first celebrant they interviewed. 'He had a fake tan and was a bit too smooth and kind of dodgy,' Vanessa says. 'He really tried to push us.' However, they eventually found a man who was 'just really nice, honest and down to earth.'

For Gail and Paul, finding the right celebrant was 'just a nightmare' which took 'twenty or so' phone calls. But in the end they found someone they liked. 'She was sort of vaguely sane,' says Gail. 'We could actually have a conversation with her. She was a nice person, calm.'

If the celebrant you have seen isn't right, don't worry about hurting their feelings—even if they look like they really need the work. Seek further. As Mum says, 'I have missed out on jobs because the couple's dog didn't like me or I've got them because another couple's dog did. Different people suit different celebrants—what's most important is finding one that is right for you.'

Ask the celebrant to provide you with contact details of satisfied clients. Geoffrey Baird always advises clients to ask a prospective celebrant, 'When is your next wedding? Can we come and watch you do it, if possible, and if the other couple don't mind'—just to get a sense of whether the person is any good or not.

Remember, there are all sorts of celebrants out there so you're sure to find the right person for you. For example, SBS Sydney broadcaster Nitza Lowenstein became a celebrant 'to offer people a proper substitute to a church or synagogue wedding'. She is renowned for beautiful civil ceremonies infused with Jewish marriage rituals. At the other end of the spectrum, Elvis impersonator Andy Seymour, of Adelaide, started offering his services at wedding ceremonies because people kept asking him if he would.

Working with your civil celebrant—what you should expect

So, you've found a celebrant who you're happy with, let's now look at what will happen in the time leading up to your big day.

The job of a civil celebrant is firstly to ensure that all the legal papers are signed and delivered to the appropriate agencies and that the legal requirements of the marriage ceremony are fulfilled. The second part of their job is to work with you to help you create and write a beautiful and meaningful ceremony. For some couples that means a very simple ceremony with no readings, extras or pyrotechnic displays. For others, it means the whole shebang—arriving in a horsedrawn carriage at the medieval village that has been created on a suburban football field and having a wedding that Merlin himself would be proud of.

Before you go to your first meeting with your chosen celebrant, it will be helpful for the celebrant if you have answered all the questions in Chapter 3. These include:

- why you are getting married and what kind of ceremony you want
- who, if anyone, you want involved in it

- what kind of music you would like
- what readings you would like
- what kind of symbolic actions you would like to undertake
- how you are going to arrive and who you are going to arrive with.

Don't worry if you haven't got a clue—the celebrant is there to help and support you in creating a ceremony that is completely your own—one that will sprinkle speckles of stardust on the shoulders of all who attend. How about that, eh?

Take the following with you:

- Birth certificates—only extracts or originals will do—in Australia. These are not necessary in New Zealand.
- Passport if you're a citizen from another country—a photocopy will not do.
- Decree Absolute if you have been married previously and have divorced.
- If you are widowed, your previous marriage certificate and death certificate of your dearly departed.
- If you are under 18 years of age in Australia, or under 20 in New Zealand, you must obtain your parents' consent and have an Order from a Judge or Magistrate allowing the marriage.

All celebrants work differently—and there are many effective ways of moulding a wedding ceremony. Following is just one example of how it can be done.

During the first meeting

- The celebrant should explain the basic elements of a civil marriage service and ask you questions about yourselves and your relationship, what you would like in your ceremony and who you would like to be involved.
- You will look at lots of material and ideas for your ceremony. The celebrant should have thick files with lots of examples of readings, vows, askings, ring ceremonies—everything. They should provide you with a palette of ideas. Or, at least, help you to go out and seek what you want. If your celebrant presents you

with only a few options that you're not happy with, then maybe find someone else.

- Some celebrants may show you a range of certificates of marriage that you can choose from—there isn't just one! If they are anything like Melbourne celebrant Judy Seregin they have an Aladdin's cave of marriage ceremonies, with shelves of books, samples of candles, ring pillows—everything you need for a whiz bang ceremony. (See Chapter 5 for more details.)
- The celebrant may ask if you would like your Certificate of Marriage to be inscribed with calligraphy.
- The celebrant will explain their fees. (More on fees later in this chapter.)
- In Australia, you will fill out the Notice of Intended Marriage form—this must be done a month and a day before the ceremony and has a life of eighteen months. You must also sign a declaration saying that there are no legal impediments to your marriage that you are aware of.
- The celebrant, in Australia, should provide you with information about pre-marriage education and give you a small pamphlet called *Happily Ever . . . Before and After.* They should also show you a copy of the celebrant's code of practice. Their job is to follow that Code of Conduct. They must also inform you about how you can make a complaint if you are not happy with the service provided. (See Chapter 2.)
- In New Zealand, the process for marrying is slightly different. You must find a celebrant before you can apply for a marriage licence. You do not need to fill out any formal documentation at your first meeting with your celebrant. This is done when you apply for your marriage licence at the Registry of Births, Deaths and Marriages.

When you sign the Notice of Intended Marriage form it all becomes that much more real. (See Chapter 2.)

By the end of the first meeting

- You should have lots of homework!
- You should have an idea about how your ceremony will be constructed.
- You should be excited and hopefully not overwhelmed.

At the second meeting

In the time between the first and second meeting, there will have been lots of correspondence between you and your celebrant. Drafts and ideas for the ceremonies should be in the process of being refined. The second meeting is really just a chance to review your progress.

By this stage, the celebrant should be able to show you a draft of the ceremony, including their introduction. You should be close to finalising your vows and askings, and anything else you want to say to each other. Readings should be finalised and you should know who is going to read what, who is going to hold the rings and so on. You should also know how you are going to arrive and how you are going to leave. After this meeting, the ceremony should only need some tweaking around the edges.

At the third meeting—the rehearsal

This is your 'dress' rehearsal. It is an absolute must. A practice run of the ceremony gives all the parties involved a chance to go through what they have to do or say and where they should stand. Whole wedding parties have been in tears during a rehearsal only to be fine on the big day. It also gives you the opportunity to road-test your water-resistant mascara. Melbourne celebrant Marita Wilcox believes that it is the job of the celebrant to:

> Make sure that every person in the wedding party knows their part. Support and encourage them until they are confident. I cannot emphasise the great importance of a rehearsal for all ceremonies. It is the rehearsal that ensures the ceremony flows without a hitch, relaxes everyone and gives the couple confidence. Most importantly, the celebrant should conduct the rehearsal in a way that gives ownership of the ceremony to the couple.

At this point, it is important that both you, your other half and the celebrant are completely clear about how the ceremony is going to run. Couples have reported occasions where celebrants have added poems or forgotten to say them because there was no master copy of the running order. In Lisa and John's ceremony, which was held on a rocky outcrop overlooking the ocean, the celebrant was supposed to ask the bride's father if he would give his daughter away. But she didn't. 'So Dad squeezed onto this rock with us, and there were three of us on this rock, with Dad getting more and more uncomfortable,' Lisa says. 'He is in every photograph and he's pulling this really funny face.' Oh dear!

One way to avoid such mishaps is to give a written copy of the ceremony—which includes what everyone is going to say and stage directions—to all the major players. Your celebrant should bring copies of this to the rehearsal. At the rehearsal, and on the big day, the celebrant may also bring copies of the readings, vows and askings, just in case someone forgets to bring theirs.

What if I am unhappy with my celebrant?

Talk to the celebrant first to see if you can resolve your problem. If you can't and you think it is of a serious nature, you can make a formal complaint about your celebrant. In Australia, contact the marriage celebrants section of the Federal Attorney-General's Department. In New Zealand, if the celebrant is a member of the Celebrant's Association of New Zealand, you can contact the association, or contact the Registrar of Births, Deaths and Marriages.

How much do celebrants charge?

There is no set fee for a celebrant's services. The Australian Federation of Civil Celebrants recommends a fee of A$350–500, but you can pay anything from A$250 to A$1000. Fees are similar in New Zealand. Additional fees may also be charged for travel time, parking and so on, but these should be agreed upon at your first meeting.

Remember that cheapest or dearest doesn't mean the worst or best. Do your research. High fees may mean 'too busy' and low fees can mean 'sausage factory'. Considering the amount of work that celebrants do, and the amount of time good ones will put into creating your ceremony, they aren't highly paid. Most celebrants have 'other' jobs—they are celebrants because they love being part of a significant event in people's lives.

When do I pay the celebrant?

Every celebrant will have their own way of conducting their business. Some celebrants ask for an initial payment up front, and for the balance to be paid at the rehearsal or on the day. Some people don't like being paid on the day as they think it detracts from the event. Discuss this issue with your celebrant.

Do I have to invite the celebrant to the reception?

No! Only if you want to.

How far in advance do I need to book?

It depends on how popular the celebrant is. Some need a year's notice, particularly if you wish to marry between September through to March as this is peak wedding season in the southern hemisphere.

CHAPTER FIVE
THE 16 ELEMENTS OF A CIVIL MARRIAGE CEREMONY

OK—you've taken that confidence pill. Now is the time to start looking at your marriage ceremony in detail. Don't be afraid. If you're worrying about what you are supposed to do—don't. A civil marriage ceremony is not unlike religious marriage services. The bonus with a civil service is that you have more creative control.

Now if you think that you don't have a creative bone in your body—don't worry. And if your embarrassment factor is high—ignore it. This book (of course) and your celebrant should help steer you in the right direction. The important thing to remember is that with you in the driver's seat, you are going to create something that is just yours—a memory that will be personal, poignant and beautiful. Precious. Trust yourself and don't worry about what you think other people will think . . .

Every aspect of the civil marriage ceremony is discussed in detail in this chapter. Some people opt for just the basics—intro, asking, vows, exchange of rings—so that it's all over in a jiffy. From where you are sitting now, this may seem attractive. BUT try to resist the temptation. You'll be amazed at how fast the ceremony goes. Many people who have been to a brief ceremony are disappointed, including the bride and groom. Everyone wants to enjoy the rite of passage that you are undertaking. Yes, we have all gone to weddings in cold, cavernous churches that have gone on and on but this is your wedding and as Mum says, 'suck it for all it is worth'.

And, yes, the prospect of standing in front of your nearest and dearest, declaring the ways in which you love your beloved can be daunting. Try not to be embarrassed about declaring publicly how you feel—your family and friends will love it as will the person you are marrying. For just a moment, think about the day after your wedding—how happy you will be, how touched your family will be, how excited all your friends will be, because the ceremony was all about you and your loved one.

A rare opportunity is in front of you. Make the most of it. Let's begin.

Outline of a civil marriage service

It helps to think of a marriage ceremony as a process of transition where you arrive as a single person, and leave as part of a married couple. The ceremony essentially ritualises your transition. It consists of four parts:

1. The invitation—where you invite your friends and family to partake in your rite of passage.
2. The asking—where the celebrant asks if you want to marry the person standing next to you.
3. The promise—where you and your beloved make promises about how you will love each other.
4. The seal—by exchanging rings and signing your marriage certificate, you seal your contract of marriage.

Most civil marriage ceremonies follow the steps outlined below. Remember this is only a sample—it's really up to you what you do and different celebrants will take different tacks.

1. The theme is chosen (if you want one).
2. The location is chosen.
3. The stage is set.
4. The music starts.

5. Your guests gather.
6. The bride and groom arrive and the ceremony commences.
7. The celebrant makes a welcome and introduction.
8. Reading—There are usually one or two readings at this point.
9. Presentation of the bride and groom.
10. Celebrant reads the Monitum—The celebrant makes a statement explaining that their role is to solemnise the marriage (this can occur after the introduction).
11. Symbolic act—This denotes the joining of two individuals in marriage, and can be anything from a sand ceremony to lighting a candle.
12. Reading—There are usually one or two readings at this point.
13. The asking—Getting down to business now. The asking is where the bride and groom say 'I do'.
14. The vows—This is the part of the ceremony where the bride and groom make public declarations and promises to each other.
15. Ring ceremony—This is where you exchange the rings and seal the deal.
16. Declaration of the marriage—The celebrant declares that you are married and the bride and groom kiss.
17. The signing—The bride and groom sign the marriage register and marriage certificates.
18. The presentation of the married couple—The celebrant presents the bride and groom with their wedding certificate.
19. Couple leave together, taking their first steps as husband and wife.

Example of a ceremony

Ceremony commences with music: 'More' by Bobby Darin. Bride and groom walk down the red carpet together and stand in front of the celebrant. Witnesses and readers stand to each side of the celebrant.

Introduction

Celebrant: In *A Room with a View*, E.M. Forster, wrote, 'It isn't possible to love and to part. You will wish that it was. You can transmute love, ignore it, muddle it, but you can never pull it out of you. I know by experience that the poets are right: love is eternal.'

On behalf of Julia and James, I warmly welcome their family and friends to this wonderful occasion of the celebration of their marriage. Both their fathers, Greg and Alan, who are watching from above, bless this union. If they had seen the relationship grow they would be absolutely delighted with the union taking place today.

We are gathered here to celebrate with James and Julia as they are united in marriage. This is a beautiful and joyous occasion because it acknowledges their commitment of deep friendship and love. As you know, this is not a new union but one that has been tested. It has matured and evolved over many years, and it is with this knowledge and understanding of each other that they now wish to publicly reaffirm their commitment to spend their lives together in marriage.

For James, his beloved Paul Weller sums up how he feels about Julia. 'I'm content just with the riches that you bring, I could run away but I'd rather stay, in the warmth of your smile, lighting up my day. You're the best thing that's ever happened, to me or my world. You're the best thing that ever happened, so don't go away.'

And for Julia, these words from 'Beloved' by Toni Morrison sum up how she feels about James. 'Paul D sits down in the rocking chair and examines the quilt patched in carnival colours. His hands are limp between his knees. There are too many things to feel about this woman. His head hurts. Suddenly he remembers Sixo trying to describe what he felt about the Thirty-Mile Woman. "She is a friend of my mind. She gather me, man. The pieces I am, she gather them and give them back to me in all the right order. It's good, you know, when you got a woman who is a friend of your mind."'

James wants to marry Julia because, apart from trying to tie her down for years, he hasn't found anyone who can make him laugh as much as she can. And for Julia, even though she finds some of James's ism's annoying, living without him would be to know despair and utter loneliness.

They both feel that marriage symbolises and formalises their commitment to each other and the future. It is also a chance, for family and friends from the past and present, to express how happy they are about this blessed union of souls.

Celebrant recites the Monitum

Reading One—A reading from the first letter of St Paul to the Corinthians

Presentation of Julia and James

After the reading, Nola, mother of the groom, and Alistair, brother of the bride, approach.

Celebrant: Who represents Julia and James here this evening?
Nola and Alistair: We do.
Celebrant: Do you, Alistair, Julia's brother, on behalf of her community gathered here this evening, give your blessing to this marriage, and do you pledge to give them your loving support?
Alistair: I do.
Celebrant: Do you Nola, James's mother, on behalf of his community gathered here this evening, give your blessing to this marriage and do you pledge to give them your loving support?
Nola: I do.

Reading Two—'Sonnet 17', William Shakespeare

The asking

Celebrant to James: James, will you take Julia to be your dearly beloved wife? Will you be committed to making Julia happy and to help her be successful and achieve all that she wants out of life? Will you do whatever is necessary to ensure the longevity of your relationship?
James: I will.
Celebrant to Julia: Julia, will you take James to be your dearly beloved husband? Will you be committed to making James happy and to help him be successful and achieve all that he

wants out of life? Will you do whatever is necessary to ensure the longevity of your relationship?
Julia: I will.

The vows

James: Julia, you are the most generous, loving, frustrating person who makes me a better person. Without you I wouldn't laugh or cry or get as much out of life. You are my biggest fan and provider of much helpful, if unsolicited and gratuitous, advice. I'm looking forward to having our family and growing old with you.

I hereby pledge my love for you, to honour and respect you, and to share my life with you. I pray that one day you will learn how to pick up after yourself. I promise to treasure our relationship, to never take it for granted, to nurture and sustain it.

I hope that my love inspires you to feel it is possible to do all the things you want to do. I look forward to our adventure together. Never forget how we feel today. I pledge to try and make it easy to remember.

Julia: James, I can't stop laughing while I'm with you. You believe that I can do all that I want to. You never make me doubt myself. I can share all my dreams and terrible secrets with you. You complete me. You are kind and generous and stubborn. One day your quest to make me a tidier person will end in your triumph.

I hereby pledge my love for you, to honour and respect you, and to share my life with you. I promise to treasure our relationship, to never take it for granted, to nurture and sustain it.

I hope that my love inspires you to feel it is possible to do all the things you want to do. I look forward to our adventure together. Never forget how we feel today. I pledge to try and make it easy to remember.

Celebrant: Julia and James, you have each made promises, commitments and pledges of love to the other. Are you prepared to accept them?

Julia and James: We are.

Celebrant: A token of the vows and commitment that are made by James and Julia here today are their wedding rings.
A ring represents eternity, unity, wholeness and commitment.
Julia and James shall now exchange rings.

Ring ceremony

Julia's aunt brings the rings forward.

Celebrant takes Julia's ring and James repeats after Celebrant:
With this ring, I wed you Julia as an outward sign of our love and pride that you are my wife.

Celebrant takes James's ring and Julia repeats after Celebrant:
With this ring, I wed James as an outward sign of our love and pride that you are my husband.

Reading Three—'Sonnet LXIX', Pablo Neruda

Declaration of marriage

Celebrant: All present here today have witnessed this marriage, and have heard Julia and James declare they will live together in marriage. They have made special promises to each other. They have symbolised it by joining hands, taking vows, and by exchanging rings. So, therefore, it is my absolute delight and pleasure on behalf of your family and community gathered here today, to declare Julia and James—Husband and Wife. Julia and James, will you now claim each other with a kiss? This is a precious kiss, the first as man and wife, that now seals the promises that you have made here today to each other in the presence of family and friends.

Julia and James kiss.

Reading Four—'Late have I loved you', St Augustine

The signing

A round of applause as the celebrant presents the marriage certificate to Julia and James.

Celebrant: I ask all of you to toast Julia and James as a gesture of your support and love as they take their first steps out into their new life as husband and wife, and may the rich love and support always be there for each other.

Music: 'Let's stay together' by Al Green

From June Newman

Now don't get overwhelmed by all the choices and decisions you seem to have to make. Don't focus on the end point. Take small steps. To get your show on the road, you need to think about the 16 main elements of a marriage ceremony:

1. Theme—Do you want one? What will it be?
2. Location—Where and when will the ceremony take place?
3. Setting the stage—What do you want the site of your wedding to look like?
4. Music—What sort of music will you have, and when will it be played?
5. Arrival of the bride and groom—How will you make your entrance?
6. Introduction—What, if any, comments do you want the celebrant or yourself to make?
7. Readings—What readings are you going to have? Who will read them and when?
8. Presentation—How do you want to be presented?
9. The asking—What questions are you going to ask each other?
10. The vows—What promises are you going to make to each other?
11. The ring ceremony—How will you exchange your rings?
12. The declaration—How will the celebrant announce that you are husband and wife?
13. The signing—How will you sign the certificate and where?
14. The exit—How are you going to make your exit?

15. Ceremony booklet—Do you want one? What will you put in it?
16. Traditions and symbols—Are there any special symbols or traditions that you would like to include?

Let's now explore each of these elements in detail.

 # 1. Theme

For some people, their wedding ceremony is an obvious place to reflect their passions.

It doesn't matter what your passion is, a good civil celebrant should be able to work alongside you and help you create a ceremony that is truly about you. If you love cars, a sport, the sea or ancient rituals, then your wedding ceremony can be woven around your obsession.

It's completely up to you how much your passion will feature in your ceremony. For example, if you love surfing, you could make a gentle passing nod to your thing by choosing a surfboard as an altar or you could make every aspect of your wedding, from invitations to reception, reflect a surf theme.

Other couples may choose a theme because they want to create something entirely different and memorable. Melbourne celebrant Judy Peiris married a couple who wanted something out of the ordinary because it was a second marriage for both bride and groom and between them they had five sons—so they chose a Viking theme. Judy says, 'They had no association with vikings, except the groom's name was Eric! The invitations were addressed, "Hear Ye, Hear Ye, Thou be officially invited to the taking of Michelle the wench to Eric the Viking."'

The celebration took place in a forest, and featured several huge (contained) bonfires and a wandering minstrel and singer. The groom wore huge ram's horns. The bride wore a Maid Marion dress and braided her long blonde hair. Most of the guests were dressed up too, in vests, ugg boots, horns and helmets, black fake fur and leggings tied with leather. 'It was wonderful,' Judy says. 'They were just an ordinary couple and they wanted a special day. And it was.'

Living your wedding dreams, however, can create some unexpected hurdles. For example, when Melbourne couple Kelly and

Michael decided to have a medieval-inspired wedding, they had to search high and low to find a park with a road through it, so a horse-drawn carriage could go right up to the wedding tent which was to be erected in the middle of the park; they had to gain permission from the local council for five tents to be erected in the park; and the rose petals intended for the ceremony perished so new ones had to be found at very short notice.

So if you are going to do something out of the ordinary, be prepared and give yourself plenty of time so that any mishaps can be dealt with. There are a number of fantastic websites that are treasure troves of ideas. For further details, see Chapter 11. Here are some examples of how couples have let their passions live on their wedding days.

A touch of Elvis

Die-hard Elvis fans in Adelaide call on the services of Andy Seymour for a wedding ceremony with a touch of the great man himself. Andy, whose registration as a celebrant is pending, with full Elvis hair and massive black sideburns, shows up to the ceremony in a big red 1971 Eldorado convertible Cadillac. When the bride walks down the aisle, he bursts into a song of their choice. Andy says, 'The most popular ones are, "Can't help falling in love", "The wonder of you", "Love me tender", "And I love you so" and "It's now or never".'

Go Team NZ

Auckland celebrant Jocelyn Fausett married a couple who were devoted supporters of Team NZ, from the America's Cup. 'They got married in a bar that was really close to the Team NZ headquarters at the harbour,' Jocelyn says. 'The cake was black and white, there were black and white balloons, and the bride wore a white filmy top and a black bra with silver ferns on it!'

Australiana

When Lisa and John married, they wanted to acknowledge their new country as John was born in Wales and Lisa in England.

Although Lisa was worried that it would seem a little cheesy, she says they wanted to do the 'whole Australiana thing'. 'I had gum leaves embroidered onto my dress. We had a Banjo Paterson reading. A friend played the didgeridoo as we left the ceremony. We are new Australians. It's a new beginning, in a new country, and we wanted to embrace that.'

Medieval

Both Kelly and Michael had always been interested in medieval life. So when they decided to marry, it was only natural that they had a medieval-inspired wedding. They created a small medieval village using five tents in a suburban park in Melbourne. All the guests, and the celebrant, wore medieval costumes. The bridal party entered with banners and formed an honour guard for Kelly and Michael, who arrived in a navy blue open carriage drawn by two dappled grey horses. The guests gathered around the wedding tent and a musician played a harp.

The ceremony also included some medieval touches. Instead of exchanging rings, Michael and Kelly exchanged favours. 'A favour is a piece of cloth that has been embroidered,' Kelly says. 'That's what we gave each other instead of rings. For us, rings have no symbolism.' They also had a handfasting ceremony, guests threw rose petals over the happy couple and there was a maypole at the wedding feast.

Example of a Shaman-themed ceremony

When Stephanie and Dylan decided to marry, Melbourne celebrant Marita Wilcox created a whole wedding ceremony infused with Shamanism—an ancient form of spirituality.

Introduction

Celebrant: Family and friends, we welcome you all here today to celebrate in the marriage of Stephanie and Dylan. Stephanie and Dylan have chosen a ceremony based on ancient ritual to reflect their commitment to each other.

The blessing

Celebrant: You continue your journey together, and begin your life of union, bound together by the vows of this rite. Your marriage is a partnership founded on the strong bonds of friendship and love, of passion and respect. Many are the years you will share and countless are the moons you will watch together. This wedding is a symbol, a celebration, and a public recognition of what already exists in the silent places of your hearts. If you keep your vows, your sacred trust, happy will be many of your days.

Candle lighting ceremony—friend lights candle

Celebrant: In this ritual today we celebrate love, and I would begin by offering homage to the eternal flame of sacred love that burns within every loving heart.

May its light guide you, Stephanie and Dylan, and bind your hearts together as one. May the fires of love kindle your passion for each other throughout your years.

Incense lighting—friend lights sticks of incense

Celebrant: Let your love be as incense to the breeze, let it create an ever growing circle that spreads love. May your union be a thing of joy and beauty to all who behold it. May you dance in the eternal spirals of time, in harmony with the cycle of the seasons, ever aware of the sacredness of life, and with the blessing of this sacred gathering.

Bell ringing—friend rings bells

Celebrant: Above you are the stars, and below you are the stones. Remember, like the heavens your love should be constant and bright, like the earth should your love be firm and bountiful. Possess one another, yet be understanding. Have patience, for storms shall come and go, and will be weathered with truth. Be free always in giving affection and warmth, for your gifts will magnify and return. And remember with compassion and joy those who have been and will be, for they are your link to eternity.

Reading

Giving away

Celebrant: Who here gives this woman to be married to this man?
Bride's parents: We do.
Celebrant: And I ask all of you present: Are you willing now and always to encourage and strengthen this marriage, by upholding both Dylan and Stephanie with your continual love and support in the years to come?
Everyone: We will.

Celebrant reads the Monitum from the Marriage Act.

Affirmation

Celebrant: Stephanie, do you desire to have this man as your husband, forsaking all others?
Stephanie: I do.
Celebrant: Dylan, do you desire to have this woman as your wife, forsaking all others?
Dylan: I do.
Celebrant: So mote it be. May the keepers of the sacred winds whisper joy into your life.

Friend rings bell three times.

Blessing of the hands

Celebrant: Stephanie, please face Dylan, and hold his hands, palms up, so you may see the gift that they are to you. These are the hands, young and strong and vibrant with love, that are holding yours on your wedding day, as he promises to love you all the days of his life. These are the hands you will place with expectant joy against your stomach, until he, too, feels his child stir within your womb. These are the hands that will comfort you in illness and hold you when fear or grief rack your mind. These are the hands that will countless times wipe the tears from your eyes: tears of sorrow and tears of joy. These are the hands that will passionately love you and cherish you through the years, for a lifetime of happiness.

Dylan, please hold Stephanie's hands, palms up, where you may see the gift that they are to you. These are the hands that are smooth, young and carefree, that are holding yours on your wedding day, as she pledges her love and commitment to you all the days of her life. These are the hands that will hold your family in tender love, soothing them through illness and hurts, supporting and encouraging them along their ways to fruition. These are the hands that will hold you in joy and excitement and hope, and console you when you are grieving. These are the hands that will passionately love you and cherish you through the years, for a lifetime of happiness. These are the hands that will give you support as she encourages you to chase down your dreams. Together, everything you wish for can be made real.

Lovely Goddess, bless the hands that you see before you this day. May they always be held by one another. Give them the strength to hold on during the storms of stress and the dark of disillusionment. Keep them tender and gentle as they nurture each other in their love. Help these hands to continue building a relationship in your grace, rich in caring, and devoted to reaching for your perfection. May Stephanie and Dylan see their four hands as healer, protector, shelter and guide.

Friend rings bells.

The vows

Celebrant: Your vows are a dedication for when you are together and when you are apart, when life is calm and when life is troubled, when you are proud of one another and when you are disappointed. Now Dylan, please speak the vows that you have written for this moment.

Dylan: Stephanie, no single set of words can contain the passion, the love and the commitment that I make to you today. By the witness of our families, I give to you the best man that I can be. I promise to be strong and to be truthful, to be passionate and excited, to be funny and decisive, to be aware and gentle, and to be yours from this day forth.

Celebrant: Now Stephanie, please speak the vows that you have written for this moment.

Stephanie: Dylan, you are the awakener of my spirit, my joy, my love, my miracle. By the witness of our families and friends, I promise to be strong and truthful, to share adventures, to bring you every happiness and to be yours from this day forth. I marry you today as I give you my heart, my body and the very breath of my soul.

Exchange of rings

Celebrant: Stephanie and Dylan have chosen to exchange rings. Tim, may I have the rings?

These rings are a symbol of the vows you have just spoken. They are the outward sign of the inner love that binds your lives together. As the ring is without seam or edge, having no beginning and no end, so it symbolises the perfection of a love that cannot end. Each ring has the cycle of the stars and the moon embodied within it. Let this cycle be yours through the wearing of these rings. Be blessed by the gods and goddesses that they may ever remind you of the vows which you have spoken today. Wear them with love and honour.

Dylan: Stephanie, will you accept and wear this ring as a pledge of my love, and as a symbol of all that we share?

Stephanie: I will. Dylan, will you accept and wear this ring as a pledge of my love, and as a symbol of all that we share?

Dylan: I will.

Celebrant: Dylan and Stephanie are now bound by love. Their unique spirit and nature will bind them closer than any written or spoken words.

Declaration of the marriage

Celebrant: Before the old gods and goddesses, and all those gathered here today in this sacred circle, let it be known that

Dylan and Stephanie are husband and wife, and henceforth shall be as one. Dylan, you may kiss the bride.

Signing of the register

Music.

Declaration and presentation of the marriage certificate

Celebrant: All present here today have witnessed that Dylan and Stephanie have accepted each other in lifelong commitment. The vows have been proclaimed, the rings have been given, the two are now as one. May they trust each other, trust life and be not afraid. May they love each other and offer love and support to those around them. It gives me great pleasure to present to Dylan and Stephanie their marriage certificate. Congratulations Mr and Mrs Brady.

From Marita Wilcox

 ## 2. Location

Location. Location. Location. Where are you going to do the deed? And when? As the sun breaks across your favourite beach or at dusk in the Royal Botanical Gardens.

The location and time of your marriage service is all up to you. Don't restrict yourselves. Is there a place where you have always wanted to get married? If you went to a religious school, would you like to get married in the school chapel? If you love the sea, do you want to get married barefoot on the sand, like Australian politician Natasha Stott Despoja did at Watego's Beach? In a castle, perhaps like Madonna? Or have you always dreamed of having a wedding breakfast?

You really can get married anywhere. But if you're not sure yet, don't worry—just think about your favourite place and go from there. And don't let all the worry worts change your mind. When they start on with the 'Why have you chosen that place?', just switch off. There are, however, some useful things to consider:

- Are there any steps? Can frail people get there? Will there be any seating?
- If you want to get married in summer, will there be any shade? Remember that if guests are looking into the sun, they will be uncomfortable. Melbourne celebrant Judy Seregin always advises clients to avoid outdoor weddings, with no shade, in the middle of summer. 'Being in the full sun for 90 minutes causes stress,' she says.
- If you want to get married on the harbour or by the sea, what will you do if the wind picks up? Wind affects sound as well; you will need the wind behind you.
- If you want to get married on an aeroplane or in a hot air balloon, make sure that you are in the air space of the country in which you are marrying!
- Is the place accessible by car/horsedrawn carriage/stretch limo/truck/skateboard? Is there sufficient parking? If inaccessible, how are your guests going to get there? Bus? Boat?
- Is there enough room for all your guests? Will they be able to hear the ceremony?
- Is it home to any animals? Intrepid celebrant Catherine Bearsley says, for example, 'Avoid a ceremony site that might be in the vicinity of a colony of bats. Their mode of communication can be an annoying distraction.'
- Is the place available?
- If you need it, is there a power outlet?

Before you go off in search of the perfect venue, log onto the wedding websites in the region where you wish to marry—the chat rooms are a goldmine of information on every aspect of weddings (frightening in itself) but inevitably you will find someone who has done the hard yards for you.

What will you do if the weather wreaks havoc?

If you are planning an outside ceremony, what will you do if the heavens open up on your big day? Panic? Cry? Get a load of umbrellas? Do a stop-the-rain-dance? Make sure you have a plan of action and, if required, set a deadline for when a decision must be made.

What is it about weddings and the weather? Many people seem to get married on the hottest, coldest, windiest day in 50 years. Either the rain could be teeming all day and then the clouds part as the band strikes up the *Wedding March*, or on a perfect day the heavens can collide as soon as a bride steps out of her limousine.

At the first wedding that Mum ever officiated, the weather meddled with the couple's best laid plans. There had been no rain in Melbourne for months. And then as the sixth of December dawned, the horsemen of the Apocalypse rode through Melbourne. It was the coldest, windiest, wettest December day for generations. But the bridge and groom were determined to marry outside with the vista of the sea in the background. She shivered in her strapless gown, while his teeth chattered, Mum's hair stood out on end and all the guests froze in their summer garb.

In South Australia, Andy Seymour worked at a wedding where the bride and groom were hell-bent on marrying at sea. On the morning of the wedding, the heavens opened. The sea was so rough the captain didn't want to take the boat out, but the bride and groom convinced him to go ahead. All the guests were saturated, but by God, they married on the water.

Remember, if you are going to be near water, it will probably be windy. It was so windy at Charlie and Odetta's wedding that Charlie's tie is in his face in every photo. The award, though, for the greatest disaster caused by weather goes to Auckland celebrant Jocelyn 'What a trooper' Fausett. Accompanied by her husband, she was the first to arrive at a wedding by a beach. There was an open-sided marquee.

A sudden gust lifted the marquee off the ground and I ended up underneath it along with my husband who got momentarily knocked unconscious! I only got a couple of grass stains on my elbow and they were easy to hide. I looked amazingly composed in all the photos, but the outcome was that I had internal bleeding from falling on one of the poles, a torn rotator cuff in my shoulder and ligament damage in one knee where I twisted around to try to avoid the falling poles! My husband had mild concussion and whiplash! I was six months in physiotherapy before I recovered totally!

So, if you are planning an outdoor wedding—as most of us do—you have to be realistic. It isn't the end of the world if you can't marry in the location of your dreams. You and the bridal party can slip out with the photographer to take photos, after the ceremony, at your dream location. Your guests won't be able to concentrate on the ceremony if they are freezing their arses off. And all they will talk about is how cold they were, not your beautiful ceremony.

When you choose a venue, think about what you could do if the weather turns. Is there any shelter? Some couples choose an outdoor venue precisely because there is a hall or rotunda nearby in the event of rain. Have a plan of action, take umbrellas, a beach umbrella or a canopy so at least the bridal party won't get wet.

In New Zealand, the marriage licence application requires you to stipulate an alternative venue in the event of bad weather. How sensible!

In your initial planning for your wedding, draw up a Plan B. Appoint people to inform guests about your decision if, on the day of your wedding, you decide to change the location of the ceremony. For large weddings, some people even hire buses to move people to alternative venues or organise a toll-free number for guests to call on the morning of the wedding.

How far will you have to walk?

You may have found the most fantastic spot but how far is the distance between where you can park and the place where you have chosen to marry? Is it a long walk? Will you be able to do it in 35 degree heat while wearing high heels and nervously clutching a bouquet? If you have decided to marry on a beach and you want the groom to wait in the ceremonial space, will you have to walk two kilometres to get to him?

Can I get married in a church and have a civil ceremony?

As a general rule, only religious marriage ceremonies can be performed in churches, temples or other religious places. There was an interesting case in New Zealand recently where an Anglican minister married his son to a Catholic bride in a Catholic church, but civil and church rarely mix in a house of God.

You will find religious people who will assist you in developing a ceremony which acknowledges your spirituality. You may even find a religious official who is prepared to assist you more directly. See Chapter 4 for further details. Alternatively, there are some non-denominational or deconsecrated and decommissioned churches, such as Old St Paul's in Wellington, New Zealand, that are drenched in the holy spirit.

When do you want to get married?

In the southern hemisphere, the majority of couples marry from September through to March. However, it's more important to choose the day, the month and time of day that are best for you.

Which day?

For some people, a particular day may be deeply significant, so is an obvious choice for their wedding day. For example, Kim and Adam decided to follow a tradition that had started with Kim's great-grandmother so they married on 18 October—the same day that Kim's grandmother and mother had both married.

Days such as New Year's and Valentine's are very popular for weddings. Just remember if you choose a popular day, make sure you book a venue and a celebrant well in advance, and if your wedding day is on a public holiday there may be some unexpected problems.

Gail and Paul encountered a few logistical hurdles caused by the fact that they wanted to marry on New Year's Day. 'Getting flowers there was a nightmare,' Gail says. 'Paul went to the flower markets in Sydney at the crack of dawn, the day before, and then transported them in a mobile cool room on the day of the wedding.'

And problems have not been confined to just their wedding day, as celebrating their anniversary has proved to be complicated as well. Gail says, 'We chose New Year's Day because we thought we would always have the day off, it would be a holiday and easy to remember. But what we didn't take into account is that most restaurants are closed on the first of January because they've all had a big night the night before, so finding somewhere for dinner has proved to be a little arduous.'

And if you are planning a Saturday wedding at a venue next to a sports field, check out the possibility of a cricket match occurring during your ceremony. Catherine Bearsley found it quite disconcerting to have loud applause during one ceremony when two cricketers were bowled out!

What time of the day?

For some couples, the time of day is one of the most important factors in making a decision about their wedding.

If you want to know when sunrise or sunset will be on your chosen day, or what the weather will be like, check out websites such as the Bureau of Meteorology of Australia at http://www.bom.gov.au/. That way you can monitor the glare factor.

Here are some examples of much loved, and successful, wedding locations.

The Old Church, Mt Tamborine, Queensland

When Larissa and Rob married, they decided to tie the knot at beautiful Mt Tamborine, behind Queensland's Gold Coast, because Larissa had spent many family holidays there and she had happy memories of the area. When they found a place called the Old Church at Mt Tamborine, they knew it was the one. 'It was one of those old timber churches, cottagey, cute, gorgeous, with little pews,' Lisa says. 'And although it was really tiny—50 people were really crammed in there—it was a beautiful place for the ceremony. It was a little bit traditional, in that it was an old church, but it was modern too because we had a celebrant.'

Monsalvat, Eltham, Victoria

Melbourne artists Amanda and Vito wanted an intimate and beautiful setting for their wedding. After some searching, they found Monsalvat. Originally an artists' colony, this large estate now houses a gallery, café and a series of impressive stone buildings, and its history appealed to Amanda and Vito. Vito says, 'We liked the feel of it. It's built along the lines of a medieval village, with lots of stonework and ornamental arches.' Before Monsalvat, the couple were considering yacht clubs because they 'both liked water views' but they were captivated by the estate's ornamental lake and so married beside it, under a large canopy. 'It was a beautiful place,' Vito says. 'We had the reflections and the sounds of the running water.'

Mount Tomah Botanical Gardens, Blue Mountains, New South Wales

Gail and Paul had always liked the Blue Mountains, just outside of Sydney, so it seemed the obvious place for them to get married. 'We'd done lots of bushwalking there and Paul had holidayed there as a child,' says Gail. 'Paul's family is from Sydney and mine is from Bathurst,' which made things inconvenient for everyone. We looked around for ages. We didn't want to get married in a church. And we wanted to get married somewhere we could have the reception as well.'

Apart from the celebrant temporarily being lost in some of the fine shrubbery, everything went smoothly and they had a wonderful ceremony and reception in a magnificent location. Also, every time they visit they are reminded of their wedding. Gail says, 'It's a beautiful garden. It was quite a young garden when we were married there and it's just getting nicer and nicer.'

Rocks above The Bower, Manly, New South Wales

Lisa and John wanted to get married by the sea and chose the rocks above The Bower at Shelly Beach—John's favourite beach and favourite surf spot. 'It's a really lovely spot,' Lisa says, 'an outcrop of rocks on different levels, with the sea below and views right up the coast. We had to get permission from the council and it cost about $25.'

The big day was 38 degrees and there wasn't much shade, and Lisa worried about how she would get up there in her high heels. But John says 'these were minor details'.

'It was a fantastic cloudless day,' Lisa says. 'Hash, our friend, played the bagpipes. Everybody said that when they heard the bagpipes fire up and it came across over the wind, they all got teary. So while Hash played, my dad and I, my bridesmaid and two flower girls walked in. Hash's bagpipes knocked the blossoms off the bushes above us, and Dad and I were laughing because Hash had no idea that we were being covered in flowers.'

Tall ship, Polly Woodside, *Melbourne*

Christine and Scott knew they wanted to be married outside. The question was where. 'With the weather in Melbourne, I didn't think it would be wise,' says Christine. 'Also, I'd been to a few outdoor weddings and I didn't like them because there was no structure; everybody would just stand around and then the bride would arrive. I was running out of places when I looked on the Internet and found the *Polly Woodside.*'

Christine went to see the nineteenth-century tall ship and knew instantly that it would make the perfect scene for their wedding ceremony. 'I loved the wood everywhere, the tall mast and the rigging. There was a covered area if it rained and it was really peaceful and it just felt like we were somewhere else.'

On the day, all the guests waited for the bride on the ship. 'I arrived in a London cab,' Christine says, 'and walked up the plank with my brother and my bridesmaid and flower girl. We had a string quartet playing on the top deck and it was just magical.'

Sunrise at Avoca Beach, New South Wales

Karen and Lachlan wanted something spectacular for the background of their wedding. As Karen says, 'What's more spectacular than a sunrise or sunset?' They decided to marry at dawn because they wanted the sun to rise behind them and over the water, and because the beach would be theirs and the ceremony more personal. Sunrise also meant that their guests were taken out of their daily routines, making the event more memorable. 'We started our new life at the start of a new day and the start of a new lunar month,' Karen says. 'It was a fresh start which really defined our trek into married life.'

Auckland Harbour Bridge, Auckland

One of the most memorable Valentine's Days that celebrant Jocelyn Fausett has had was on the top of Auckland Harbour Bridge where she performed a ceremony for an English couple who wanted to do something that was uniquely Auckland.

'We all had to put on grey jumpsuits and chain ourselves to the bridge,' Jocelyn says. 'There were nine media people and about five for the wedding party. Fortunately it was a fine day. We did the whole walk from one side and got up to the top and did the service up there.' And, because of safety regulations that ban anything that flaps about or is not attached, Jocelyn had to have the service papers laminated and tied around her neck on a ribbon. 'One of the guides carried the bouquet up in his backpack and the bride had her hair done up with little white flowers,' Jocelyn says. 'Of course, because it was so noisy, we had to use the tour group intercoms for the service.'

Kennedy Point Vineyard, Waiheke Island, New Zealand

Canadian couple Jackie and Murray wanted a small and intimate wedding. They chose Kennedy Point Vineyard because, Jackie says, 'It was really beautiful with a view of the vineyard and of the bay.' It was also completely private and perfect for tiny weddings—Jackie and Murray's ceremony had just the bride and groom, the Justice of the Peace and the two vineyard owners as the witnesses. 'It was 100 per cent stress-free because we stayed in the guesthouse on the vineyard,' Jackie says, 'and simply walked into the backyard of the guesthouse for the ceremony.'

Marrying overseas

Many couples love the idea of escaping to a tropical island or the other side of the earth, either with or without their families. There are some legal considerations if you do this (See Chapter 2 for more details). If you do decide to marry overseas, there are lots of companies that can help you. The best way to start is by looking on the Internet, as many companies such as hotels, resorts and tourism agencies, specialise in weddings and advertise their services there. You could also attend bridal fairs in the country of your choice or use the many international bridal magazines.

Nga Hau e Wha National Marae, Christchurch, New Zealand

British couple Dianne and Steve chose to marry abroad, having been to a friend's wedding at the Sydney Opera House in 2000. 'We had always wanted to visit New Zealand as various friends had commented on what a beautiful country it was,' Steve says. 'So we thought, why not, and decided to get married in New Zealand.'

Steve cruised the Internet for the websites of New Zealand wedding organisers and found Donna Dohi from NZ Dream Weddings. 'She replied almost immediately and was extremely informative,' says Steve.

With Donna's help, Steve and Dianne chose a Marae-style wedding at the 'Nga Hau e Wha National Marae' in Christchurch. The couple arrived at the wedding in a Rolls Royce, and were welcomed with a traditional Maori Warrior Challenge, followed by a fairly straightforward marriage ceremony. 'We spent the evening in a fabulous hotel overlooking Christchurch square and the following afternoon in Kaikoura, swimming with a pod of hundreds of dolphins, which was a lovely way to start our honeymoon.'

Steve says that the morning after their wedding, he and Dianne awoke to a rather large surprise—they were on the front of the local newspaper. 'Donna, who had been brilliant throughout, had informed us that our wedding at the National Marae was a first for a couple from overseas and, if we would agree, the *Press* (which is the largest daily paper in the South Island) would like to report on it. We agreed because we thought it would be a small insignificant article somewhere in the middle of the paper, if they chose to print it, not on the front page! And we also had a bigger feature article than Tony Blair [UK Prime Minister] and his election campaign.'

Town Hall, Venice

Australian-born Sarah and her Danish husband, Tommy, married at the Town Hall in Venice. They were living in Sweden at the time and were keen to marry but unsure as to how they could bring their families together from opposite sides of the earth. They decided to combine a holiday with Sarah's sister and husband in Italy, with a marriage ceremony. They also asked Tommy's mother if she would like to come on a 'holiday' with them to Italy. They called the Town Hall in Venice and spoke with representatives from the Danish and Australian embassies.

'We told my sister and her husband and Tommy's mum, Connie, what we were up to on the way to the Town Hall of Venice on the morning of the wedding,' says Sarah. They were married by the very serious Mayor of Venice and then went out and had a wonderful lunch.

Some months later they returned to Australia and had a wedding party on a Sunday afternoon in Sarah's Mum and Dad's garden with friends and family, replete with a renewal of vows ceremony. 'It was lovely,' recalls Sarah.

Five star hotel, Fiji

When Rebecca and Cameron met, they were both divorcees with children from previous marriages. They decided that it was all too complicated to marry in Australia so opted to have a wedding in paradise in a five star hotel. 'It was better than we ever imagined,' says Cameron. 'It was just the kids, Rebecca and me.' They married in one of the beautiful gardens of the hotel while a band played. 'Rebecca carried a pineapple and I wore a Hawaiian-print shirt. The girls dressed up as fairies and two strangers were our witnesses. It's a great memory,' says Cameron.

Alkmaar, the Netherlands

When Marianne and Dave decided to marry, they chose to tie the knot in Marianne's home town in the Netherlands. Following Dutch custom, on the morning of their marriage, Dave, wearing an Akubra hat and Aussie-flag socks, went to Marianne's parents' home with a bouquet of orange and eucalyptus flowers. Then, with all their wedding guests, they walked through the neighbourhood to a canal where a boat was waiting to take them to the medieval town centre. 'We sipped champagne and watched windmills turn as we glided past,' Marianne says. 'But the bridges were so low, we all had to bend under them!'

When they docked, Marianne's brother pushed Marianne, Dave and their small daughter Kim in an old-fashioned cart covered with pillows, ivy and balloons through the town to the Town Hall which was built in the 1100s. The ceremony was in Dutch and English, with a Registrar of Marriages replete in traditional gowns, and Dave and Marianne also exchanged words they had composed for each other. When the ceremony finished, the town bells rang out!

3. Setting the stage

You've got the perfect spot, and you've chosen the big day, now, how are you going to create the right kind of atmosphere?

When you walk into a church or religious place, you walk into another world. Altars, candles, statues, paintings, leadlights, the smell of incense and beeswax all create a sense of being out of the ordinary, and heighten the sense of occasion. Obviously, this is not the time to bring in the builders (mind you, some grooms and brides have) but your ceremonial space should be special.

Take a mental picture of your proposed field, mountain top, local hall or outdoor garden. Try and imagine how it will look on your wedding day. Take off the rose-coloured glasses—is there anything that stands out that may need some attention? For example, are there toilets? Is it in the middle of a high-traffic area? How are the bride and groom going to get from the car to the ceremonial space?

You hold the brushes and pots of colour when it comes to setting the scene. Try not to think of it as just another chore, try to think of it as exciting—a chance to attain your vision, however large or small that may be.

Looking back, Julia wishes that she had put more effort into the finer details of her wedding ceremony. 'At the time I was tired,' Julia says. 'There was just so much to do and Mum said that she would do the flowers to decorate the large old fountain around which we were marrying. They were fine, but she used a series of native flowers which I actually didn't like and I wish I'd been bolder and thought about it more—I would have liked to do something out of a Baz Luhrmann film. Gerberas—perhaps. Ribbons. Something Bollywood. But I needed to come up with the idea and trust myself and care more about it, and I didn't.'

Creating your ceremonial space and atmosphere is not supposed to make more stress for you. It should be fun, and achievable. This is not the time for control freaks and 'bridezillas'; this is the time for planning, and for some help. Unless you don't mind using a mallet and getting down and dirty in your wedding gown, you're going to need the helping hands of others to execute your vision. Besides, your family and friends will love to help.

Here are a few essentials for setting the scene:

Define the space

Outdoor weddings are becoming more popular, but you must have a definite space. Some spaces are already defined for you and ready-made for weddings—such as the Women's Memorial Garden in the Melbourne Royal Botanical Gardens which is sunken and walled, or the rotundas and bandstands that are in most public parks throughout Australia and New Zealand. All these spaces lend themselves perfectly to wedding ceremonies.

An open field, on the other hand, is just that. And if it's a public place you will need to claim your ceremonial space and define it. This doesn't mean that you have to spend months crafting the perfect arbour, like the Owen Wilson character in *Meet the Parents*. A simple scattering of rose petals or flags fluttering in the wind are just as effective.

You can source your props at bridal fairs, where you will find merchants who hire out canopies, arbors covered with flowers, chandeliers, candelabras and so on. Or search the Internet. Celebrants can also be a source of props and ideas.

When Karen and Lachlan married by the ocean on Avoca Beach at sunrise, their canvas was a glorious stretch of sand. To define their ceremonial space, six bamboo flares were placed in the sand, on the morning of their wedding, in the dark of pre-dusk, and these created a path that led to a small wooden platform which a friend had made for them. The temporary platform meant that Lachlan and Karen were slightly elevated, and, decorated with flowers, it signified the importance of the area.

Create a focal point

A focal point is important because it directs the eye, it adds a layer. In all houses of worship, there's a focal point. Even in a nightclub, the focus is on the desk of the deejay. It doesn't have to be religious or even ceremonious. Choose something that is about you. If your ceremony has a theme perhaps there is something appropriate you could use.

Kath and Stuart created an altar for their wedding with a surfboard and Kath's bikini, towel and sun cream draped across it. Those things represented, for them, the qualities of freedom, strength, dedication and endurance which Stuart and Kath regarded as essential qualities of their lives. On the surfboard there was also a bouquet of flowers which represented the blossoming of Stuart and Kath's love and the creation of their family. There was also a certificate that officially welcomed Kath's child, Christopher, into the groom's family.

Other couples choose a focal point which is more traditional, like a table decorated with ceremonial or significant items such as flowers and candles. Or your location may provide a focal point, such as a fountain in a garden.

Julia and James created a very personal focal point for their ceremony. To acknowledge their fathers, who were both deceased, James and Julia placed large photos of each of them on a small table close to the celebrant. James says, 'We wished that they were there and in some ways they were. They appear in all the photos of the ceremony, which is kinda funny and really lovely.'

Make sure that everyone can hear

If you want to avoid guests cupping their hands over their ears and loudly whispering, 'What did she say?' throughout the ceremony, get a microphone so that all your guests can hear clearly. People cry at weddings because they are overwhelmed at how beautiful the bridal party looks, or how moving the declarations of love are. Grannies want to hear what their lovely grandchildren are saying. It's such a shame if your guests can't hear properly. You don't need to employ one of Kylie's roadies. A simple microphone, fed through a battery-operated stereo system with an output, will do. Make sure you test it and the batteries work too.

Some celebrants don't use microphones, some use one and some use two—one for the bridal party and one for the celebrant. Those celebrants that use microphones typically have their own public address systems which they have been known to lug up hill and down dale. Your venue may already have such facilities, so make sure you check.

What kind of atmosphere do you want?

Now that you have defined your space and created a focal point, you can start adding the details such as music, actions, lighting and smells. These elements add to the drama of the occasion, making your wedding ceremony more memorable.

Music

Music has a vital part to play in creating an atmosphere so make sure you use it. Imagine your ceremony starting with Billy Idol's 'White Wedding', or with Wagner's traditional *Wedding March* or with a friend ringing bells or a man in a velvet hat playing a lute. Music creates different feelings. Strike your note.

Melbourne celebrant Marita Wilcox officiated at a wedding where an acapella singer began singing as the bride and her father approached the focal point. The singer was somewhere in the crowd and not easily seen. Then another singer, in another position, joined the first, then a third and a fourth. 'At this point the bride and father were in the middle of the guests in the aisle. The singers all came forward to meet the bride and father and lead them to their positions,' Marita says. How beautiful it must have been for the audience.

For more information, see the next section about element 4— music.

Lighting

There are two types of light—natural and artificial. If your ceremony is outdoors, you need to think about the time of day and the time of year. Sometimes there can be too much natural light and many a celebrant has tried to coax out guests hiding in surrounding bushes because the blazing midday sun is too piercing. If your ceremony is to take place indoors or at night, then you can play with the lighting to create all sorts of visual effects if you desire.

At another ceremony conducted by Marita Wilcox, lighting was manipulated to great effect. It was an evening wedding and music was playing as the guests waited for the bride and father of the bride. As they approached, the music stopped and the lights went out. A trumpeter played in the darkness for a few moments. Then a pink spotlight shone on the bride and father as they walked in. As they reached the guests, another spotlight, coloured blue, shone on the groom. 'Finally,' Marita says, 'as the bride stood beside the groom, the two colours merged together to form a new colour.'

Action

As you arrive, there is an opportunity, if you desire, to enhance the moment with some gestures or actions. Actions are the symbolic connection between yourselves and your loved ones. They highlight what you are doing. When Marie and Joe married, the bride arrived in a Cadillac then five couples lined the route to the altar and as Marie passed each one, the couple raised a decorated hoop and blew bubbles!

When Emily and Roger married in a medieval-themed ceremony, the guests assembled in a semicircle. As the couple arrived, a circle of rose petals was placed on the ground. Bells were rung and a cup of mead was passed around the group. Rose petals were cast over the couple as the celebrant said:

> Let your love be as petals to the breeze, let it create an ever growing circle that spreads love and may your union be a thing of beauty to all who behold it. May you dance in the eternal circle of time with the dance of the earth, with the sacredness of life and of this sacred space (Kingma 1991).

Smell

You don't have to mess with the natural aroma of what is already there. Others like to arouse the senses further by burning incense or lighting some scented candles, or these may be part of the ceremony's ritual. Moderation is always best, however, as some of your guests may be allergic to your favourite aromas.

Take your places please . . .

Also consider how you are actually going to do the getting married thing. Where is the bridal party going to stand? Where do you want the celebrant to be? A lot will depend on the size of the group and the location, as well as the couple's wishes. There are a number of options, but it's really important that the focus is on the couple and the bridal party and not on the celebrant. Discuss it with your celebrant during your meetings and work out what is best at your rehearsal.

And where are you going to sign the register? If you don't want to flash your rack to all and sundry, it is advisable to sit down on a chair at a table. Great photos are also captured when you and your lovely sit down to sign on the dotted line. Allocate someone to look after a table and chairs—some celebrants may see this as part of their charter but many don't (they simply haven't got enough arms, what with the PA, the journals, the ceremony and the rest). Make sure you insist on a style standard—you wouldn't want your magnificent atmosphere ruined by two smelly camping chairs and an old table covered in bird poo.

Don't forget that pregnant women and elderly or infirm guests would probably like to sit down so make sure they have chairs. If required, look at your guest list, work out how many are going to sit down and then go from there. Try and choose chairs that won't sink into the ground; ones that fit in with your vision.

How are you going to coordinate all this, plus be the bride or groom? For some venues, you may not be able to access your place until an hour before your big moment—do you have a crew that can bump you in and out? Contrary to your opinion, you may not be able to do everything yourself, so make sure you enlist the assistance of friends and family. Appoint a trusted person as the stage manager so that all the parts of your ceremony fall neatly into place.

 ## 4. Music

Music is the rhythm of life. Don't underestimate the power of music. A ceremony without it is dead because music is our core and represents every aspect of the human condition. Music can dictate emotions. It is a very powerful tool. Movies are rarely made without music because music manipulates us. It plays with us, reinforces feelings and creates an atmosphere.

In an interview in the *Sydney Morning Herald*, Australian

broadcaster Margaret Throsby explained the power of music. On her daily national radio show, she interviews guests and asks them to select five pieces of music that have personal meaning. 'Many guests are surprised, and sometimes embarrassed, to find themselves revealing far more than they intended, even shedding tears' (Javes 2004).

Throsby believes it's often the music, rather than her questions, that triggers the tears:

> Sometimes they haven't heard the song for a long while or it reminds them of a loved one or a difficult time. It happened just recently with jazz singer Dianna Krall. She chose the duet of Bizet's 'The Pearl Fishers', music she listened to as a child, and was quite discomforted when she became emotional. Journalist Paul McGeough shed floods of tears listening to the 'Flower Duet' from *Lakme*, music he used to listen to in Afghanistan around the time his colleagues died in an ambush.

While we don't want all your guests sobbing, music has power. Use it. A Tom Jones classic played a critical role in the courtship and marriage of Lisa and John. The first time John took Lisa back to his place, he played his favourite song, 'Just Help Yourself' and got Lisa up to dance and sang it to her. Aww—who said romance was dead? 'I fell in love with him then,' Lisa says. Later on John proposed to Lisa at a Tom Jones concert in Melbourne when Tom sang that very song and, 'We put a verse from the song on our wedding invitation and it was our bridal waltz. It's kind of like our seminal piece.'

Whatever music you choose—whether it is live or recorded—just make sure that you and your guests can hear it! If you have live music in an open space, it may not project at all. Who wants to watch a mime artist at your wedding? Sound please!

Music is usually required for at least four parts of the ceremony:

The prelude

This is the music that will set the scene. Select music or instruct musicians to play for at least 45 minutes in case you're late!

Processional

This is the music that will play as you walk down the path to marriage. In the olden days, 'Here Comes the Bride' (the bridal chorus from *Lohengrin*) was used. At last year's wedding of Prince Frederik of Denmark to Mary Donaldson, Mary chose 'Fill thou my life, O Lord my God,' a Scottish hymn, for the arrival of the Donaldson family, and for her own arrival 'Zadok the Priest' by Handel was the track of choice (www.hkhkronprinsen.dk 2004). Choose a piece of music that is at least three minutes long to make sure that unexpected hazards, like a grandmother stepping in front of the bride to take a photo because she thought she would never live to see such an event, are taken into account. Pachelbel's *Canon* is very popular as it is suitably grand and lasts at least six minutes. Melbourne celebrant Judy Seregin's favourite track is 'Here I Am' from the Disney movie *Spirit*, 'as it just builds and builds.' 'Everyone gets quite emotional when they hear it,' she says.

The signing

The signing can all be done in five minutes; however, if your photographer wants to capture lots of special shots, you may be signing for a whole lot longer. Choose music that goes for at least 15 minutes.

Recessional

This is the music for the conclusion of the ceremony. The whole day is about this moment. Make the most of it. People generally go for something joyous and uplifting—'Chariots of Fire' or James Brown's 'I Feel Good', or Al Green's 'Let's Stay Together'. Choose whatever feels right for you.

In general, with music, go with what you like. Don't judge yourself or ask yourself, 'Is this appropriate for a wedding?' It's your wedding. It's about you and what you like.

Again, there's an endless number of wedding websites out there, with lists of suggestions, MP3 downloads, song sheets—seek and you shall find. See Chapter 10 for some suggestions for songs—with thanks to many music websites.

5. Arrival of the bride and groom

The ceremony starts the moment the bridal couple appears. Your arrival is the opening act. It creates a sense of anticipation that something magic is going to unfold. There are so many props, such as music, instruments, lights, flowers, smoke machines, bubbles or flags that you can use to heighten the sense of occasion. Princesses have rows of trumpeters heralding their arrival. Flower girls can spread rose petals to create a path for the bride. Incense sticks can burn a path to the ceremonial space.

There are as many ways to get to your wedding as names in the phone book. Most couples choose something with wheels, hooves or paddles. One celebrant arrived at a wedding on the back of a camel! Anything goes.

Catherine Bearsley, a celebrant from New Zealand who is now based in Victoria, officiated at a wedding on an island where the bride and groom arrived by water taxi and were greeted by a friend playing the piano accordion. 'The couple then walked, hand in hand, to their ceremony space, with the guests all following behind,' Catherine says. 'We certainly felt like "their village".'

If you're thinking of arriving on a horse to your wedding, Pat Lane, a celebrant from north-eastern Victoria, has this sage advice: 'When a bride decides that she wants to arrive on a horse, it's not a good idea to ride side saddle unless she is well used to riding this way. Bridal gowns can be protected by placing a large white rug over the horse.' Pat also says that you must make sure that the horse can cope with a crowd of people and the chosen music, especially if bagpipes are involved, as well as the general noise and excitement of a wedding.

Once you're onsite, what do you do then? There's no right or wrong when it comes to walking down the aisle. Maybe you don't want to walk that long aisle alone. Maybe you do. The golden rule is—do what you want and what you feel comfortable with.

The traditional road

Traditionally, the best man and the nervous groom would wait for the bride to walk down the aisle with her father. This was Dad's big moment—he would stand to your left and walk, or in the case of the

Earl of Spencer, wobble, down the aisle with you. For Lisa, it was really important to her that her father gave her away. 'My Dad really wanted to and I really liked that,' she says. 'As much as it was a modern wedding, I think that it was my Dad's moment and I didn't want to deprive him of it.' Gaby, however, didn't want her father to give her away because she 'really wanted to avoid all those traditional, masculine sort of macho things.'

There are many variations on this theme. These days brides go it alone, take their mothers or anyone else who is significant to them, be it their brother, best friend, child or dog. Don't laugh—celebrants have the scars to prove it.

Marita Wilcox conducted a wedding where the father of the bride and the bride walked in to beautiful slow music. 'Then, as they reached the guests, the music changed and the father and daughter started dancing—a bit ballroom, a bit jazz. They danced down the aisle to their place at the ceremony. And while they were doing that, all the attendants danced on the spot.'

Bride and groom walk together

At many modern weddings, the bride and groom walk down the aisle together.

When Julia and James married, it seemed to make sense that they would arrive together. Julia says, 'We'd been together for a long time. It just seemed the only thing to do. My father was deceased. And to ask anyone else would have created all sorts of problems.' They married in the garden on the grounds of an historic reception centre. They appeared at a doorway together and walked down a stretch of red carpet, around a fountain to the ceremonial space.

Bride and groom greet guests

In this popular version, the bride and groom get to the ceremony not only on time but before everyone else and then greet guests as they arrive. This is how Gaby and Marcus started their wedding. 'We went before the ceremony to greet everyone,' says Gaby. 'It really shocked people but it was great because it calmed us down. We didn't want to be just hanging around while our guests arrived, waiting, waiting, waiting, and then be driven up last to the ceremony.'

Do I have to hold a bouquet?

No. You don't have to. However, flowers, leaves, anything is good because it gives your hands something to do.

I'd like everyone to have champagne before the ceremony starts . . .

What a lovely idea. But what if you're late, some of your guests get tipsy and the inner hecklers come out of the closet during your ceremony?

6. The introduction

This is where it really starts. How you kick off is up to you. You can say nothing and just get into the nitty gritty or you can explain how you and your loved one started on the road to love and why you have decided to marry.

Traditionally this is where a priest or minister would say, 'We are gathered here today to celebrate the marriage between . . . and . . .' In a civil ceremony, this is where the celebrant welcomes everyone and outlines the history of the relationship between the bride and groom and why they have decided to take this great leap of faith.

The introduction can contain:

- An official welcome to all present on behalf of the couple and their families.
- An explanation of why the couple have chosen to be married.
- An account of how the couple first met, what they liked about each other, how they fell in love, what the courtship was like, who proposed to who and when it took place.
- An explanation of what their family and friends mean to the couple.
- How the couple will strive together to make their union work.
- How the couple will keep their relationship rich and vibrant.

Melbourne civil celebrant Clive Rumney believes that information about how a couple first met plays an important role in the ceremony. He says, 'It is not only an excellent way of ensuring that the ceremony is personally tailored for each couple, but it often also creates an opportunity to inject some humour into it.' Clive believes that humour creates a friendly atmosphere and if the couple laugh at themselves, it helps them get over wedding jitters.

The introduction to your wedding ceremony can be short and sweet, or long and deeply significant. It can be funny or serious. It's up to you. Here are some examples of introductions:

History with a touch of humour

Celebrant: I'm sure that many of you will be aware that Nicki and Ranil have now known each other for about eighteen months. I gather that the initial step in the process that led to them meeting was when Ranil went to a store to buy some furniture. Sandra, Nicki's mother, sold him the furniture. A few days later, Ranil met Sandra again in a park while each was walking their dog, and through this contact he subsequently met Nicki when she was also walking her dog. The rest, as they say, is history. Sandra, we live in an age where we often hear of retailers offering special deals and free give-aways to make their customers happy. I'm sure that the give-away you'll be making in a couple of minutes was not what you had in mind at the time. *[At this point Sandra interjected by saying, 'Who said it was free?']* But nonetheless, I think you can draw immense satisfaction from the fact that buying furniture from you has certainly made one customer very happy indeed. This gathering applauds you for that.

We are here now to write a new and very special chapter in the history of Nicki and Ranil. I am sure that I speak for everyone here when I say that we hope there will be many, many more long and happy chapters in that history. And in case any of you are wondering, the family dogs Sheba and Charley also get on very well together.

From Clive Rumney

Statement about love and commitment

Celebrant: We have come together today to witness the joining of two lives. Andree and Angelo are best friends; they are soul mates. They stand before us today, strong and committed to each other, ready to face life together as a married couple. They stand before us knowing that through the private commitment of their hearts and the open proclamation of their vows, they are embarking on a life that binds them inextricably to each other and to the family they have lovingly created.

They have chosen to openly declare their love for each other and celebrate their happiness before you, their closest family and friends. You are an integral part of their day-to-day being; you are the loving and supportive community that strengthens their lives.

Good afternoon everyone. It is with pleasure that I warmly welcome you on behalf of the bride and groom. Angelo and Andree are very pleased that you are here to share this important occasion with them.

From Judy Seregin

A prophecy for success

Celebrant: I don't know if any of you believe in omens. I suspect that we're probably more inclined to do so when we see them as good ones. Well, on my first visit to see them I saw an omen which says something quite wonderful about the sense of friendship and understanding which exists in Michelle and Tim's home. Some of you will know that they have a fish tank. Two of the residents of that tank are a black ghost knife fish and a clown loach—which are, of course, two entirely different species of fish. Yet these two are obviously the very best of friends. We're not talking about any interspecies hanky panky here; just two fish that are so very comfortable in each other's company that, at night, when all fishy activity in the tank had stopped, they were resting very contentedly with each other, the black ghost knife fish leaning comfortably against the clown loach. This being on the night that I was there to discuss their wedding plans with Tim and Michelle, I had to hope that this serves as an omen for the strength of their relationship, and for the comfort that they will continue to draw from each other's company.

From Clive Rumney

Friends will be there to support you

Celebrant: Don't walk in front of me, I may not follow. Don't walk behind me, I may not lead. Just walk beside me and be my friend forever . . . Albert Camus

Milly and Jon you have come here today to this space you have created to celebrate your wedding as two separate and unique individuals, bringing your own special qualities, talents and personalities. You stand amidst the warmth and security of your closest family and friends, your community, who are united in their affection for you both and in their desire to see you live a happy and fulfilling life together. It is within their shelter and within their care that you have grown and will continue to grow as individuals and as a loving and committed couple. Their presence here confirms the significance of your relationship and adds support and strength to the marriage you will commit to. If it is your sincere intent to be united in marriage, join hands and begin to walk life's path together. As you do, draw strength from the strong emotion and goodwill that surrounds you and from the caring and supportive people who have gathered to wish you well.

From Judy Seregin

Groom seeks permission to marry the bride

At this wedding, the groom regretted not asking the father of the bride for his daughter's hand in marriage so when they arrived next to him at the altar, he did.

Groom: Angus, thank you for accompanying Meredith to be by my side today, I have always regretted that I did not officially ask you for your daughter's hand in marriage, so today before our marriage, may I have your blessing?

Luckily Dad said yes!

From June Newman

How the couple first met

Celebrant: As many of you will know, Jane and Scott have now been together for eight years. They actually owe their meeting to a train cancellation. Jane was on her way home from uni. And when her usual train didn't run, she caught the next one, the one that Scott was going home on. I'm told that it was probably Jane who was the first to see the other. Her interest, and sense that 'this could lead to something special', was immediate. So much so that instead of getting off the train at her station she went through to the next one. And what was Scott doing during this fateful journey? Although ostensibly looking out of the window, he was actually using the reflection to watch Jane watching him. I understand that they didn't actually speak to each other then, but the foundation was laid, and the friendship which brings us all here today started shortly after.

Jane and Scott, as you told me this story I thought of an old saying. It is one that I hope will serve as a good omen for your future life together, for it is often used to characterise 'determination', 'dedication' and 'willingness to make a great effort'. That old saying is, of course, 'going that extra mile'. Jane, you initially did that literally, but the fact that you are here now, having declared your wish to marry, shows that you have both figuratively 'gone that extra mile' for each other; and are prepared to do so for the rest of your lives. I am confident that I speak for everyone here when I wish you well in this important endeavour.

From Clive Rumney

Symbolic acts

After a brief welcome, civil celebrant Cherie Scott led this introduction which incorporates symbolic acts:

Celebrant: Elizabeth and Andrew have come here today to freely offer their gifts, to make public their love for each other, to announce their truth, to declare their choice to live and partner and grow together—out loud and in your presence, their friends and family. Andrew and Liz's desire is that you will all bear witness to their decision and share your love and support with them, now and in the days to come.

They hope also that this ritual of bonding will help bring us all closer together in community friendship and love. If you are here with a spouse or partner, let this ceremony serve as a reminder of your own love and bond. Andrew and Liz are entering into this marriage with the awareness that as individuals everything in life, all the love, insight, wisdom and power, all the knowledge and all the understanding, all the nurturing, all the compassion, and all the strength resides within themselves. Therefore, they are not marrying each other in hope of getting these things, but with the intention of giving these gifts, that the other might have them in even greater abundance.

They see marriage as a place of opportunity. One that allows for the true and honest expression of all that is highest and best within them, including their love of life, love of work, love of God, love of people, of creativity and all aspects of their being which bring them joy in life.

Celebrant: I would like to begin by lighting a candle. The candle or the flame is a universal symbol of love and of the human spirit, of the light within and without. God is different things to all people, so as I light this candle please have it represent whatever God or the highest means to you, or your highest aspiration for humanity.

Also of symbolic importance, we have on this altar two candles burning which represent Andrew and Liz and their individual pasts, and the wedding candle, which shall be lit later to represent their future together. A small broomstick symbolises their home and family life, which they will later jump over, as a sign of moving together into their future. A plate of foods and a cup of water represent the elements of physical life and nature which sustain and nurture our physical bodies. With these offerings we invoke a blessing from the Earth energy to witness this joining this morning . . .

By the roots for a strong foundation for this relationship
By the stems for standing firm and proud

By the leaves to grow and prosper together
By the flowers for joy and laughter
By the fruits for a long and enduring relationship.

Elizabeth and Andrew then take the plate and feed each other in turn, saying: 'May your hunger be satisfied'.

Elizabeth and Andrew then take the cup, handing it to each other, saying: 'May your thirst be quenched'.

Celebrant: Life is a sacred journey and this day is a celebration of a union and a new beginning. It is also a significant rite of passage that includes and celebrates the journeys that Andrew and Liz have taken which have brought them to this point.

   The story of their meeting is one of romance and magic and conjures the image of a dance—like the tango perhaps or the courting dance of two exotic birds—where the male and female, whilst eyeing each other intently, circle each other as if warily. They dance apart for a time, before being magically drawn together, never to be parted.

At this point the celebrant tells how Andrew and Liz met, before continuing the ceremony.

From Cherie Scott

 ## 7. Readings

Your selection of readings and music can really make the ceremony your own. They also offer opportunities to include people who are special to you.

Do I have to have readings?

No.

What sort of readings should I choose?

The choice is endless. Find something that is meaningful for you. Don't judge the source. If the lyrics of Metallica do it for you, use them. Readings do not have to come out of your high school great dead English poets text. There is nothing worse than going to a wedding ceremony that doesn't seem to be about the bride and groom. If you are a metal head, embrace it and share it because that is you. If you are the secretary of the local Jane Austen society, go for it.

If you come from a religious background and your parents or other family members are disappointed that you are having a civil ceremony, why not choose something that is familiar to them? A reading from the Bible, such as the first letter of St Paul to the Corinthians 12:31 – 13:8, may go down well. If you come from a different culture, perhaps you could include a reading to reflect your heritage?

How many should I have?

Two to three readings is a good number as they give the ceremony some light and shade.

Who should I choose to do the reading?

Choose people who are special to both of you, and try to match the reading to the person. So, no soppy love poems for the stiff upper lip and no hilarious readings for the wee church mouse.

It is better if the celebrant doesn't read—who wants to listen to someone who doesn't really know the couple droning on for the whole shebang anyway?

I'd like to include a lot of people in my ceremony

This is a great chance to do that. If you choose a long piece, you can ask a number of people to read a few lines or verses each.

What if I don't have anyone to ask?

Of course you do. All your nearest and dearest are on the tips of their toes waiting for you to ask. Even though you may not think so, everyone loves weddings and everyone loves to be involved. In fact, you may have the opposite problem with all the pushy scary control freaks that you are related to trying to muscle in on your ceremony any way they can—if so, be brave and resist, resist, resist. It is hard because you don't want to offend people, but you must claim your day as your own. Don't ask. Tell. And pray!

Can I mention God?

Of course you can—throughout your ceremony if you want.

Where do I find readings?

Your celebrant should be able to provide you with suggestions. Get on the Net. We all have favourite songs, novels, poems, quotes that we've read—search your soul and you will find. See Chapter 10 for some suggestions for readings and poems.

I can't find anything, what should I do?

Keep looking! Or write something yourself, or get a friend to write something about you as a couple. Some very surprising and touching words can be revealed. (Although some really awful poetry can be composed with the best of intentions and this may require tact.)

 ## 8. The presentation of the bride and groom

In religious marriage services, this is the part where the minister would say, usually to the father of the bride, 'Who brings this woman to marry this man?' These days some couples skip this part altogether— or they use this part of the ceremony for other purposes, such as for the parents of the couple or for their children to express their support of the union. This part of the ceremony also lends itself to a symbolic act such as lighting candles. Following are some ways to present the bride and groom:

Presentation of bride and groom to representatives of each family

Gaby and Marcus chose to begin their presentation by formally asking their families to accept each other and to light candles symbolising their acceptance. (These candles were also used later in the ceremony, when Gaby and Marcus used them to light a candle to symbolise their new life together.)

Celebrant: Bob and Kath, do you present Marcus to be married to Gabrielle and do you receive Gabrielle into your family?
Bob and Kath: We do.
Celebrant: Tracey, on behalf of Marcus's family, please step forward and light this candle to symbolise your acceptance and support of this union.
Celebrant: John and Phyllis, do you present Gabrielle to be married to Marcus and do you receive Marcus into your family?
John and Phyllis: We do.
Celebrant: Isabel, on behalf of Gabrielle's family, please step forward and light this candle to symbolise your acceptance and support of this union.

From Gaby

Presentation of bride and groom from friends or witnesses of the ceremony

Some couples prefer to keep this part of the ceremony informal and simple. Ange and Jack wanted to involve their friends . . .

Celebrant: Dan and Cass, as special witnesses to the bride and groom, do you happily bring them today to be married?
Dan and Cass: We do.
Celebrant: And I ask all of you present, are you willing now and always to encourage and strengthen this marriage, by upholding both Ange and Jack with your continual love and support in the years to come?
Everyone: We will.

From Marita Wilcox

Each parent says a few words

Rather than have a traditional presentation, Leona and Chris asked their parents to each say something. This included the step-parents of the bride as her parents had divorced and remarried.

Celebrant: A traditional part of the marriage ceremony was that the bride was 'given away' by her father. We don't do this much now, as times have changed. But instead, Leona and Chris wish to acknowledge and honour the special role played by their parents in their lives to this point. They greatly value the advice and support that their parents give in enriching their day-to-day lives and have asked them if they would write something for today. In a very special gesture now, you are about to hear how Sandra and Ross, Pam and Barry, and then Steve and Sharon responded to this request. I invite Sandra or Ross to speak first.

Sandra: Ross and I give our blessing to Chris and Leona and the commitment they are making today. We love them dearly and encourage them to support one another to be the best that they can be. We wish them happiness and joy as they enter marriage and the pleasure of getting to know each other for the rest of their lives.

Celebrant: Pam, would you care to speak next on behalf of yourself and Barry?

Pam: I remember Chris when he was two
He used to welcome me home with arms wide
It's not only Chris but the rest of us too
That welcome Leona to be his bride.
Whilst we live across the world in Messing
We are here today to give our blessing.
We wish you both all the very best
and lots of happiness for your future lives together.

Celebrant: Steve, Chris's Dad, will now speak on behalf of himself and Sharon.

Steve: Sharon and I are very proud and happy to be part of the very special moment as you embark on the next part of your journey through life together. Our wish is that your lives continue to be happy, fun and most of all filled with love, honesty and respect for each other. You deserve the best life has to offer, so reach for the stars and always remember, we promise to help you along the way with our love, support and encouragement as you grow in your relationship as a couple and as individuals.

From Clive Rumney

 ## 9. The asking

This is the 'I do' part of the ceremony. With the asking all you have to do is make definite statements followed by definite responses. You don't even have to say the same things to each other, but you can. What you say is up to you.

The most common way of reciting askings is for the celebrant to ask you each a series of questions and you reply with an 'I will' or 'I do'. Alternatively, the celebrant asks you both, at the same time, a question or questions and you both reply, 'We will' or 'We do'.

A traditional asking would be something like 'Do you Marlena take John to be your lawful wedded husband?' but many couples choose askings that are more personal. Here are some examples but remember that a celebrant can help you to write your own.

Examples where couples ask the same things of each other

Emily and Luke

Luke, will you take Emily to be your lawful wedded wife? Will you aspire to love her and live together in a spirit of tolerance, mutual support and concern for each other's well-being, sharing your responsibilities, your problems and your joys? Do you aspire to help and support each other to continue to provide a loving stable home for your children; to cooperate in bringing them up to be caring, honest and happy people?

Fiona and Anton

Anton, will you take Fiona to be your lifelong partner? Will you take her as your only love from this day forward? The one you laugh with, live for, dream with and love?

Martina and Tom

Tom, you have taken Martina to be your friend, your wife and life companion. Will you lovingly support Martina's dreams, hopes and goals? Will you stand by her through whatever may come? Do you promise to openly share your life with Martina, to speak truthfully and lovingly to her, to accept her as she is and delight in who she is becoming? Will you always be there to comfort her in her sorrows and rejoice in her victories?

Examples where couples ask different things of each other

Brenda and Norm

Norm, will you take Brenda to be your lawful wedded wife? Will you love and respect her, be honest with her, put up with her mood swings and stand by her through whatever may come so you can genuinely share your life together?

Brenda, will you take Norm to be your lawful wedded husband? Will you love and respect him, be honest with him, put up with his mood swings, with him being out at the cricket club or the races, and stand by him through whatever may come so you can genuinely share your life together?

Harry and Jake

Harry: When my eyes first glimpsed you from across the room, I felt my heart flutter. In all the time that I have shared with you, my feelings for you have not wavered, so today before all of our collective friends and family I declare: You are my chosen one, You are my love, I promise to remain faithful to you for the rest of my days.

Jake: You mean everything to me, I thank my lucky stars to have met and fallen in love with you. Today before my family and friends I promise to stand by you through thick and thin until death do us part.

Celebrant: Harry and Jake say one after another: I take you for my partner for life, through ups and downs until we part, to meet again at our final resting place.

Celebrant: Do you Harry and Jake accept these promises?

Harry and Jake: We do.

Examples where the celebrant asks the couple together

Lynelle and Tony

Celebrant: Lynelle and Tony, do you promise to love, support and respect each other with kindness, consideration and loyalty, and give up the errors of your ways?

Lynelle and Tony: We do.

Phill and Scott

Celebrant: Will you, Phill and Scott, listen, comfort and nurture each other?

Phill and Scott: Yes.

Celebrant: Will you stand by each other no matter what may cross your path?

Phill and Scott: Yes.

Celebrant: Will you remain faithful to the pledges you have made to each other today?

Phill and Scott: Yes.

 ## 10. The vows

Your vows are the public statements that you make about the passion and love that you feel for each other and will be carrying into your future life together. Vows are very personal.

The exchange of vows is the part of the ceremony where you make promises to each other, so try to make ones that you can keep and are meaningful to both of you. You can adapt what is typically said in a religious service or you can write your own. There is no reason why both partners have to say the same thing. It is totally up to you.

Some people don't like to veer from the traditional vows. And others want to take the opportunity to personalise them. Whatever you choose, remember that vows don't have to be completely serious but they must come from the heart and reflect the essence of who you are.

If you're writing your own, here are some questions that may get the creative juices flowing:

* What is the funniest thing that your beloved has done?
* What is the kindest thing that she/he has ever done?
* What is the thing that she/he has done that is most memorable?

How long should vows be?

They should be as long as you want. They don't have to be of similar length or content. Size does not matter. Sincerity does. And passion.

Remember that some of us are far better at spilling our feelings and sharing them with a group than others. We can't turn into something that we aren't. So if your husband/wife-to-be is a person of few words, don't expect them to wax lyrical about you. Treasure the few words that they share.

Should you tell them to each other before the ceremony?

Again, it's up to you. Some couples don't tell each other, others write their vows together.

Is there anything you have to formally say?

No. The vows are the declaration that comes from your heart. It's the declaration of your love for your partner and the expectations you have for your life together.

Do I have to say 'love and obey'?

If you want to say this, go ahead; if you don't, don't.

'Till death do us part'?

For some of us, promising that you love your partner forever is taken for granted. Others may want to try to love their partner forever but don't feel able to make that promise. You must do, and say, what feels right for you.

Traditional vows

Vanessa and Richard chose a traditional vow as they thought it summed up exactly what they wanted to say. There was no need to mess with it.

Richard: I, Richard, take you Vanessa to be my wife; to have and to hold, from this day forward, for better or worse, for richer or poorer, in sickness and in health, to love and to cherish, as long as we both shall live. This is my solemn vow and promise.

Macy and Thorne's 1995 wedding (from TV show 'the Bold and the Beautiful')
Macy: Today our lives will be joined in perfect harmony; the music which unites us comes not from our voices, but from our hearts. You have shown me time and again that, together, we are strong enough to defeat anything that threatens to come between us. I promise now to always believe in the strength of our love, and our commitment to one another . . .
Thorne: Here in front of everyone we love, I give you everything that I am—my dreams and my fears, my triumphs and my failures. I trust you, Macy, and I will always endeavour to be worthy of your trust in me. If we face times of struggle and hardship, you can depend on me to support and protect you—no matter what the cost . . .

Celtic wedding vow

You cannot possess me for I belong to myself
But while we both wish it, I give you that which is mine to give·

You cannot command me, for I am a free person
But I shall serve you in those ways you require
and the honeycomb will taste sweeter coming from my hand

I pledge to you that yours will be the name I cry aloud in the
night and the eyes into which I smile in the morning
I pledge to you the first bite of my meat and the first drink from
my cup
I pledge to you my living and my dying, each equally in your care

I shall be a shield for your back and you for mine
I shall not slander you, nor you me
I shall honor you above all others, and when we quarrel we
shall do so in private and tell no strangers our grievances
This is my wedding vow to you
This is the marriage of equals. (Llywelyn 2002)

Earth vow

Ideally, these vows should be spoken outdoors while standing under
a tree or near a lot of vegetation. If indoors, large potted plants and/
or potted trees should be brought in to frame the couple as they
speak. The vows can be repeated back to the celebrant; or the couple
can speak them back and forth to each other.

By seeds of all beginning, I make this oath.
By the roots of all depth, I swear to love with all my might.
By the stem and trunk that reach the sky, I swear to respect
your soaring spirit.
By buds that grow, I swear to never crush your dreams.
By leaf that kisses the sun and rain, I swear to share my joys
and sorrows with you.

By flowers that opens to the dawn, I swear that I do trust you.
By fruit that gives forth sweetness, I swear to nourish and
support you.
By seeds within the fruit that grows the tree anew, I swear to
begin anew with you, again and again,

As many times as the gods shall decree.
By life and death, by Lord and Lady, by hand and eye, by heart
and spirit,
This I do swear to you here before the Fates
And mark my soul forever with your touch.
As all green things grow, so shall our love,
As its memory be carried forever beneath the feet
Of a thousand generations to come. (Kaldera and
Schwartzstein 2004)

Examples where couples say different words to each other

Ange and Jack

Jack: Sweetheart, my TV has been tuned to channel Ange for
the better part of 10 years now. In that time we've shown that
we can do anything and everything together—except perhaps
sport, because you're actually pretty unco.

We have a lot in common and always have a lot of fun
together, but we both know that it's often our differences that
make it interesting for us. We are opposites in many ways and
this only serves to make us better people. We balance each
other out, complete each other. We have our fair share of
arguments of course, but we always work things out and in the
end we're better for it.

I promise I will always be there for you, look after you,
protect you and be sympathetic when you curl your bottom lip
and ask me to do things in that croaky voice of yours. I will
encourage you in all that you do and help you live life to the
full. I will soothe you when you are afraid. Settle you down
when you're a bit hyper and pep you up when you're down.

I will try to make sure that, in our lives together, we
continue to strike a balance between work and play—that we
do the hard things to achieve the things we want to achieve,
but at the same time enjoy life and not take it all too seriously.

This is why I love you, this is why I want to marry you, why I
want to grow old with you and this is why I'm excited about our
future together.

Ange: Jack, when I started to think about what I would say to you at this moment, I kept thinking about a song that always makes me think about you. It really sums up all that I could ever want in a partner and exactly what you've always meant to me. So I thought I'd share it with you and with everyone here tonight.

The song's called, 'O Somebody' by Depeche Mode.
'I want somebody to share, share the rest of my life,
Share my innermost thoughts and my intimate details.
Someone who'll stand by my side and give me support
And in return, he'll get my support.
He will listen to me, when I want to speak
About the world we live in, and life in general,
Though my views may be warped, they may even be perverted,
He'll hear me out and won't easily be converted
To my way of thinking, in fact he'll often disagree,
But at the end of it all, he'll understand me.

I want somebody who cares for me passionately,
With every thought and with every breath.
Someone who'll help me see things in a different light,
All the things I detest I will almost like.
I don't want to be tied to anyone's strings
I've carefully tried to steer clear of those things,
But when I'm asleep, I want somebody
Who will put their arms around me and kiss me tenderly.'

Jack—you have always been all this to me and more.
You make me laugh when
I'm feeling completely blue.
And I smile every time I look at you.
I am so very happy and proud to be marrying you.

Michelle and Derek

Derek: Michelle, you are God's precious gift to me, my springtime, my hope and my joy. You are everything that's good and pure and true and I worship you with my mind, body and soul. How blessed I am to be able to say that you are mine, to be able to love and cherish you for the rest of my days. I vow to be there for you always; when you fall I will catch you; when you cry I will comfort you; when you laugh, I will share your joy. Everything I am and everything I have is yours, from this moment forth and for eternity.

Michelle: Derek, as we meet here with our family and friends, I pledge my love to you, and invite you to share my life as I hope to share yours. I promise to walk by your side as your best friend, your lover and your soul mate. I will share your laughter and tears and promise always to respect you as an individual and to be conscious of your needs, and to let you free on a Saturday between the hours of 1.30 to 5.30 p.m. I promise to support your dreams and to be there for you for all of our lives.

Kate and Mike

Mike: I, Mike take you, Kate, to be my wife. I promise to share my life openly with you. To care for you in sickness and in health. To provide support in raising your son James, and to keep your feet warm as long as there is heat left in my heart.

Kate: Mike, with you I have learned to laugh again. And I have dared to dream of a bright future. I promise to give you the best of myself and ask no more than you can give. I shall share in your dreams and comfort you in your sorrows. I look forward to our future and for us to grow old together. And . . . I promise to keep your heart warm provided you keep my feet warm.

Megan and Jamal

Jamal: Megan, I bring you the gift of love; a love that accepts you; a love that treasures you; a love that comforts you; and a love that sets you free. With this love, I stand before you to offer my honesty, my companionship, my respect and my commitment. There is no one who can take your place; who can give me so much warmth, dignity and courage; who can speak to me, listen to me and understand me; and who can grow with me. I want to be all of this to you. The richness of our journey together is beginning. I give you love.

Megan: Jamal, I bring you the gift of peace; a peace deep inside that grows so calm, yet so strong; that forms a human bond so rich and fulfilling to ease past sufferings and to let your spirit fly. With this peace I share with you your dreams and visions, your struggles and your loss of loved ones who cannot be reached and who cannot be present today. I look forward with courage to the life that lies before us; to give freedom and respect; to nurture understanding; to listen; to be always sensitive to our cultural histories and to venture out to those unknown boundaries. Most of all I look forward to sharing with you the beauty of life around us. I give you peace.

Summer and Liam

Liam: I, Liam, take you, Summer, to be my partner. I will stand by you through our future, respecting you as a person, your individuality, your needs, your changes. I will support you in your quest for satisfaction and development and will work hard to solve problems and enhance our friendship and intimacy throughout our lives.

Summer: Liam, I promise to be your lover, companion and friend. Your ally in conflict, your comrade in adventure. Your consolation in adversity, your accomplice in mischief. And your associate in the search for enlightenment.

Sheridan and Justin

Justin: Sheridan, I promise to love you, support and encourage you until my soul has left my body. I look forward to building our relationship with hard work and tenderness and I promise to seek help when I need it. I am at my most vulnerable with you and promise to always be this way. I promise when the surf is up or the trout are biting, I will always put your needs first. As there will always be another wave and another trout, but never something as amazing as you, Shen.

Sheridan: Justin, I want to share my life with you, I love you for yourself, and I want you to become all that you can be. I promise to respect you as an individual, and I intend to develop as a person in partnership with you. I will love you

through good fortune and adversity, and I promise to honour
this pledge.

Brenda and Norm

Norm: As we come here today to celebrate our marriage, I ask
everyone here, our children, our family, our friends, to witness
that I, Norm, take you, Brenda, as my wife. I will love you and
will look after you. I will respect our children and give help to
them in need. I will care for all our pets. I will try to bring you
happiness and laughter throughout your life. Whatever our
future may hold, Brenda, I love you, I need you and I promise
to be a good and faithful husband to you as long as we both
shall live.

Brenda: As we come here today to celebrate our marriage, a
marriage is a commitment between two people, spoken
publicly before witnesses. And so, Norm, I commit myself to
you today before this gathering of family and friends, without
reservation or embarrassment of any kind as I say, I love you, I
need you and I promise to be a good and faithful wife to you,
as long as we both shall live.

Examples where couples say the same things to each other

Kim and Adam

I ask you Kim/Adam to love me unconditionally through
whatever life may bring. No matter what fate sends our way, I
need to know that you will respect my individuality and stand
by me as my wife/husband.

I, Kim/Adam pledge to you Adam/Kim, my love and my
trust. I promise to be ever faithful and honest, to share my
fears and hopes, to seek your help in troubled times. I
promise to be true to myself and to you, never sacrificing
my beliefs just to please you, yet never placing myself above
our love.

I give you this ring as a symbol of the love that will be
forever in our hearts.

Tom and Simon

Tom: I wish to share with you a life of tolerance, trust, respect and good humour, and having made these promises to you, I take you today to be my lifelong companion whatever life may hold for us, and as a symbol of this love and trust I give you this ring.

Same response from Simon.

Lance and Michael

Lance: I am proud to announce in public that I, Lance, take you, Michael, as my lifelong partner. To share with you a relationship of love and tenderness and laughter. I will stand by you through all our tomorrows, respecting your individuality, your needs, and your changes and promise to enjoy your love throughout our lives.

Same response from Michael.

From Norman Knipe

Soul Mates

I take you to be my wife/husband. I come here today to join my life to yours, before our friends and family. In their presence, I pledge to be true to you, to respect you, and to grow with you through the years no matter what we may encounter together.

I take you to be my wife/husband. I invite you to share my life as my partner, my supporter, my friend and my lover. I promise always to respect your needs and accept you as you are. I promise to honour this pledge as long as I live.

Today I marry my friend and soul mate. The one I have learned from and shared with, the one I have chosen to support and encourage. Our relationship has been built up with trust and honesty and I promise to share with you my heart and soul. I promise to always love, honour and respect you through laughter, tears and through this lifetime of adventure together.

I, take you to be my wife/husband. I invite you to share my life as my partner, my supporter, my friend, my lover. I will do everything I can to maintain our love. I will talk to you and listen to you. I will give to you and take from you. I love you for yourself and I want you to become all that you can be. Our love is very special and I will always love you, my friend.

From Jocelyn Fausett

Vows with a hint of Elvis

Lucky: I, Lucky, take you Rusty, to be my wife and partner.

As your husband, I promise to love you and be your teddy bear.

Because tigers play too rough, and lions ain't the kind you love enough.

I will be your strength and your big hunka love.

I wish to share with you, an intimate relationship built on trust, and to love you tender.

I promise to be open and honest with you. I'll never treat you like a fool,

Or treat you mean and cruel, for I don't have a wooden heart.

I prayed I'd never get a hard-headed woman,

And you've made me king of the whole wide world—but just don't step on my blue suede shoes baby!

I will stand by you through our future together, keeping you dry from that cold Kentucky rain, until we find peace in the valley.

Rusty: I, Rusty, take you Lucky, to be my husband and partner. I thought you were a hound dog, cryin' all the time,

But now I know, you are my teddy bear. Wise men say, only fools rush in, but I can't help falling in love with you. I want to share my life and world with you,

Because I'm stuck on you.

I want to share with you, an intimate relationship so I can love you tender and be your good luck charm.

I promise to be open and honest with you,

And, my deepest thoughts I will share with you, because it's now or never. I will help you to fulfil your goals and dreams, and I will always treat you nice. I will stand by your side through our future together, respecting and honouring you, with love and support, until we find peace in the valley.

With thanks to Andy Seymour, Adelaide, Elvis impersonator and celebrant-in-waiting.

 ## 11. The ring ceremony

The rings are the only physical symbols you take away from the ceremony that signify something incredible has taken place. You arrived at your ceremony as a single person and you leave as part of a married couple. The flowers will wilt, the food will be eaten, the wine will be drunk and the dress will be put away. However, the ring on your finger symbolises to yourself and the world that you are now part of a couple. Therefore the ring ceremony is deeply significant and shouldn't be rushed.

The ring will become a part of you and will remain on your hand for the lifetime of your relationship. Your hands will age and your ring will wear but the symbolism that it embodies will remain.

The ring ceremony offers you a chance to stop talking and undertake a meaningful symbolic act. If you wish, this part of your ceremony provides the opportunity for anyone who is important to you to take an active role.

Do you have to use rings?

No. Some couples exchange objects such as earrings. Others, if they are medieval enthusiasts, exchange favours—pieces of embroidered cloth. When Tommy Lee married Pamela Anderson, they dispensed with rings and had tattoos marked on their ring fingers.

How should the rings appear?

Again, it's up to you. They can sit in the best man's pocket, or rest on specially made ring pillows or ring bears. Or they can sit on the altar on lotus blooms. Celebrant Judy Seregin has a friend make up exquisite ring pillows. Discuss what you want with your celebrant.

Before the rings are exchanged, friends or family can bless them by taking the rings in their hands and making a silent wish or a public statement. Alternatively, a group of friends or family can circle the couple and pass the rings from one person to another, in a ring warming ceremony. Here are some examples of ring ceremonies:

Ring warming ceremony

This can be a great way for people who are special to you—particularly children—to play an active role in your ceremony. In the example below, two children who were very dear to the couple had the task of giving all the guests the opportunity to bless the wedding rings. The children took their job very seriously.

Celebrant: Marriage is a state in which two people come together and create a union that is greater than the mere sum of two individuals. It is difficult to express in words the profound relationship that is love. The ring is the symbol of your love and regard for one another.

From time immemorial, the circlet of metal has been an emblem of the sincerity and permanence of a couple's love and regard for one another and their union. As the precious metal turns again upon itself, so does a good marriage turn upon itself for its refreshment and renewal. This ring is the symbol of the commitment which binds these two people together. Take these rings and exchange them in the spirit of love.

Before these rings are exchanged by Pauline and Thierry, I call upon Ben and Ruby to come forward. Ben and Ruby will carry the rings amongst you. This will give you an opportunity to touch and bless the rings, and transfer your blessings and good wishes to the rings. As Thierry and Pauline wear these rings, they will carry your thoughts and good wishes with them forever.

The children go to each guest who in turn bless the rings. The ceremony continues with the placing of the rings on the fingers, etc.

Celebrant: From this day forward the wearing of the rings will be a spiritual union between all gathered here today and Pauline and Thierry. As everyone here has touched the rings, you have left your blessings, your goodwill and love on the rings. This will be carried through to Pauline and Thierry in their journey of life together. The ring is the symbol of the commitment which binds Pauline and Thierry together. These rings mark the beginning of a long journey filled with surprises, laughter, tears, celebration, grief and joy. There are two rings, because there are two people, each to make a contribution to the life of the other, and to their new life together. May these rings glow in reflection of the love which flows through the wearers today.

From June Newman

Ring ceremony with a 'Lord of the Rings' flavour—Lord of the Rings J.R.R. Tolkien

Celebrant: Three Rings for the Elven-kings under the sky,
Seven for the Dwarf-lords in their halls of stone,
Nine for Mortal Men doomed to die,
One for the Dark Lord on his dark throne
In the Land of Mordor where the Shadows lie.
One Ring to rule them all, One Ring to find them,
One Ring to bring them all and in the darkness bind them
In the Land of Mordor where the Shadows lie.
This is the Master-Ring, the One Ring to rule them all.
This is the One Ring lost many years ago . . .

Kids come out.

Celebrant: Uh oh . . . what's this? Two little hobbits bringing two precious rings? . . . Ah but this is not the precious! . . . These are the rings to bind those present . . . these are the Yegles rings . . . the rings of marriage of Tony and Lynelle . . . these rings are the symbol of their new bond, which like a circle never ends. OK, hand the right ring to the right person kids!
Tony: I give you my precious ring, as a sign of my promise and a symbol of my love.

Lynelle: I give you my precious ring, as a sign of my promise and a symbol of my love.

Celebrant: The rings are a symbol of the vows you have just spoken. As the ring is without seam or edge, having no beginning and no end, so it symbolises the perfection of a love that cannot end. May they remind you of the vows which you have spoken today. Wear them with love and honour.

From Marita Wilcox

The power of the circle

Celebrant: The symbolism of the circular rings was captured by the American Indian leader Black Elk, who said: 'The Power of the Worlds . . . in a circle. The sky is round, and I have heard that the earth is round like a ball and so are all the stars. The wind in its greatest power whirls. Birds make their nests in circles . . . The sun comes forth and goes down again in a circle . . . Even the seasons form a great circle in their changing and always coming back again to where they were. The life of a man or a woman is a circle from childhood to childhood, and so it is in everything where power moves.'

Celebrant prompts and Daniel says: Melanie, I commit myself to the bond and unique relationship that exists between us, and pledge to keep it alive. As this ring has no end, neither shall my love for you.

Celebrant prompts and Melanie says: Daniel, I commit myself to the bond and unique relationship that exists between us, and pledge to keep it alive. As this ring has no end, neither shall my love for you.

From June Newman

The significance of a gold ring

Celebrant: The act of giving and receiving of rings reminds us that love itself is an act of giving and receiving, the most that life has to offer. These golden circles are the natural symbols of enduring love. They represent an inward belief and trust in togetherness. They represent an outward sign of spirit and commitment, signifying to all the bond of marriage the two of you share.

Marcus, as you place this ring, as a visible sign of your commitment in marriage, on the third finger of Gabrielle's left hand, please repeat after me . . .

Marcus: Gabrielle, please wear this ring, and the world will know that I am yours and you are mine.

Celebrant: Gabrielle, as you place this ring on the third finger of Marcus's left hand, please repeat after me . . .

Gabrielle: Marcus, please wear this ring, and the world will know that I am yours and you are mine.

From Gaby

Rings attached to flowers

When Jaclyn and Jim married, each of the wedding rings was tied, by a florist, to the centre of a gerbera flower.

Celebrant: Words are powerful, but fleeting, and the sound of them is soon gone. Therefore, the wedding ring becomes the enduring symbol of the promises we have just heard. The ring is round, like the round of the year, summer, autumn, winter, spring and summer again, for in marriage we must weather all seasons.

Flowers handed to Jim and Jaclyn.

As you take the ring from the flower, place this flower within your own heart; love it, keep it safe, and give it light; and may it bloom forever from this day forward as you exchange your rings.

Jim: As a symbol of how endlessly happy you make me, Jaclyn, I give you this ring, my dear sweetheart, so you and the whole world will know how much and how always I will love you.

Jaclyn: Jim, thank you for this beautiful ring, I accept it as a symbol that I belong with you. This ring will remind me of you, I will wear it with love, all my life.

Jaclyn: As a symbol of how endlessly happy you make me, Jim, I give you this ring, my dear sweetheart, so you and the whole world will know how much and how always I will love you.

Jim: Jaclyn, thank you for this beautiful ring, I accept it as a symbol that I belong with you. This ring will remind me of you, I will wear it with love, all my life.

From Judy Seregin

Tattooed ring ceremony

Of course, you don't even have to have wedding rings—Pam and Tom had their rings tattooed on their fingers.

Celebrant: A wedding ring is a symbol of unity, a symbol of a loving relationship, a circle unbroken, without beginning or end. For centuries, men and women have exchanged rings made of precious metals in their marriage ceremony.

Instead of a gold ring, Tom and Pam have had etched onto their fingers an indelible reminder of their vows.

Pam, please hold Tom's hand and look upon that permanent ring as he repeats his vows . . .

Tom: This ring that encircles my finger is a symbol of my promise to you to make our life one; to create a good and happy life for us and our children. I love you and I am proud to be your husband.

Pam repeats the same words.

From Judy Seregin

A reflection on our future

You really can do anything that you like. When celebrant Catherine Bearsley married Catherine and Peter, they made the following statements to each other after they had exchanged rings, before the declaration of their marriage.

Catherine: I will accept you as you are, bear with you, be there for you, constant in my love, my tolerance and my advocacy.

Peter: I will appreciate you as you are, laugh at your jokes, admire your accomplishments, acknowledge your efforts, praise you to others.

Catherine: I will defend you against those who would be your detractors and act as your friend and your advocate.

Peter: I will have patience with your process, let you do it your way, show you that I believe in your ability to get it right and be there to applaud.

Catherine: I will honour your choice to grow or stay the same, leaving you space for solitude and for people.

Peter: I will allow you room for thoughts and opinions and tastes that we may not share. I will trust you and honour yours in me.

Catherine: I will listen to your story as you tell it to us both in all its variations.

Catherine and Peter together: This will be the balm to our souls. I will love you and give thanks for you all the days of my life.

 ## 12. The Declaration

Basically this is the part of the ceremony where the celebrant says that you are now husband and wife and you smooch. Lips puckered please! Of course, the declaration can contain whatever you want, but it's usually fairly short. Listed below are some examples of declarations of marriage made by those who have trodden the road before you.

Example 1

Celebrant: On behalf of everyone gathered here, I extend to you our love and support. May your relationship strengthen throughout a long and happy journey together. May you be the sharers of dreams, consoler to each other's sorrows, and helpers to each other in all of life's challenges. May you encourage each other in whatever you set out to achieve. And may you inspire each other until the end of your days. Congratulations, you are now married! Ange, you may kiss the groom!

Example 2

Celebrant: All present here today have witnessed that Lynelle and Tony have accepted each other in lifelong commitment. The precious rings have been given; the vows proclaimed; the two are now as one. As Leunig says: 'Love one another and you will be happy, it is as simple and as difficult as that. There is no other way.' I now, on their behalf and on behalf of the community, declare them to be partners in crime . . . I mean partners for life. You may now kiss each other.

Example 3

Celebrant: To all here that have witnessed what has taken place both in body and spirit, I now proclaim you, Melissa and Dave, husband and wife. Melissa and Dave, seal your promises with a kiss.

The married couple hold hands forming a complete circle.

All: We swear by peace and love to stand, heart to heart and hand in hand, Mark, O'Spirit, and hear us now, confirming this our Sacred Vow.
Celebrant: This sacred rite of marriage ends in peace, as in peace it began.

Example 4

Celebrant: May your hands forever be clasped in friendship and your hearts forever joined in love. Inasmuch as you have been bound by your will, your intent and your vows, in the presence of your family and friends, it gives me great pleasure to now pronounce that you are . . . husband and wife. You may now kiss.

All examples from Marita Wilcox

13. The signing

The signing of your certificate is very straightforward. It is where you make it all official. This is also the moment that your photographer and guests will want to capture on film. This part of the ceremony is quite short but most people have special music playing at this time as taking photographs can be quite lengthy. Champagne may be served at this time as well and then everyone can toast the couple.

Once the documents have been signed, the celebrant presents the certificate to the couple and declares the marriage ceremony complete. Most people have a small table set up for the signing, with flowers, a special pen, a candle and two chairs. Your celebrant may provide the table and special pen but they may not, so find out.

Catherine Bearsley never uses a fountain pen for a signing, after a tragic experience early in her celebrancy career. A sudden wind and rain squall came through a wedding ceremony just as the happy couple signed their papers. Not to be daunted, the couple determinedly held their position until fat rain drops began to land on their freshly signed—with a fountain pen—papers. In haste, all retreated under a large tree. 'It was then that I noticed the wondrous ink patterns on the marriage certificate,' recalls Catherine, 'and the blots on the third page of my brand new register.'

Also, make sure the celebrant knows what to say when they present you with your marriage certificate. The celebrant usually says something like, 'I would now like to present Mr and Mrs . . .' but if you don't want to be a missus, or if you do, make sure you tell your celebrant. You don't want to cause confusion in the first few minutes of your married life!

In Australia, there are three documents that you have to sign. They are:

1. The certificate of marriage—a copy which you keep for yourselves—it is not your official marriage certificate.
2. The certificate of marriage, issued with a serial number, and with a statutory declaration that you have made on the back. The celebrant will send this to the Registry of Births, Deaths and Marriages so that your marriage will be officially recorded. It is considered your legal marriage certificate.

3. The celebrant's register. This is a journal that your celebrant is legally required to maintain. It simply records the details of your marriage.

    In New Zealand, you have to sign two copies—one for yourself and one for the Registry of Marriages—your celebrant is responsible for sending this copy to the registry.

Choices with the marriage certificate

You cannot design your own marriage certificate. However, the marriage registries, plus a number of other companies and organisations, have a range of designs for you to choose from if you wish to veer from the standard certificate. Your celebrant may also have a selection. (Contact your Registry of Births, Deaths and Marriages or the Australian Federation of Civil Celebrants.) If you wish, you can also ask for all the 'infill' in your certificate of marriage to be done in calligraphy. Your celebrant should be able to organise this for you.

Signing as a symbolic act

Some couples choose to make the signing a feature of the ceremony. Before Lynelle and Tony were presented with their wedding certificate, their friend Guy read a piece that was special to them . . .

Celebrant: Friends and family, your attention please. Before I present Lynelle and Tony with their wedding certificate, I would like to welcome back Guy who will read a piece which is special to Lynelle and Tony.

Guy: Like Earth . . . know balance . . .
Like Wind . . . fly free . . .
Like Fire . . . be alive . . .
Like Water . . . feel peaceful . . .
Celebrate Your Life and Enjoy the Journey!

Celebrant: Thank you to all and may the blessing of Elves and Men and all Free Folk go with you. May the stars shine upon your faces!

From Marita Wilcox

Jumping over a broom

After Emily and Roger signed all the documentation they joined hands as a sign of union and together jumped over a broom to mark the beginning of their union together.

Celebrant: In true marriage lies
Nor equal or unequal; each fulfils
Defect in each, and always thought in thought,
Purpose in purpose, will in will, they grow
The single pure and the perfect animal,
The two-cell'd beating, with one full stroke, Life.
Alfred, Lord Tennyson (1809–1892) (Not very medieval but lovely nonetheless!)

From June Newman

 ## 14. The exit—presentation of the bride and groom

So you've made it to the end. Here is an example of what your celebrant can say at this stage:

Since you have consented to join together in the bond of matrimony, and have pledged yourselves to each other in the presence of your family and friends, I now pronounce you partners in life. Congratulations.

You're finally married—let the party begin! Now that the ceremony is over, how will you exit the scene? There are many options for a spectacular finale. Melbourne cosmetics queen Natalie Bloom got the surprise of her life when, at the conclusion of their marriage ceremony, her husband produced an unsaddled 64-year-old elephant to carry them away (Gross 1999).

At a ceremony that celebrant Catherine Bearsley devised for Cate and Ashley, they were faced with a venue that banned the throwing of confetti, rice or rose petals in or around the grounds. Cate and Ashley therefore decided to emerge to the sound of bells.

Catherine says that bell ringing is significant across many cultures, such as the Irish wedding tradition where the chime of bells is thought to keep evil spirits away. 'Cate's mother and her friends cleaned and ribboned fourteen hand bells of all sizes and shapes,' Catherine says. 'With a little organisation and with much laughter and energy on the part of the women, Cate and Ashley did indeed emerge into sunshine and happiness.'

Saskia and Toby

When Toby and Saskia married, they departed their ceremony with a nod to the navy. As many of the bridal party were navy men, two of them formed an honour guard for the bride and groom:

Best man: Many naval customs and traditions, regardless of nationality, have survived through the ages and are shared by sailors around the world. In that time-honoured tradition Toby will now walk Saskia under the Arch of Swords formed by Chief Petty Officer Quartermaster Gunner A and Chief Petty Officer Quartermaster Gunner B.

Swordbearers draw cutlasses and turn the blades to the wind. Toby and Saskia walk to the arch. Swordbearers lower swords.

Uncle Skipper: The right of passage is a kiss.

Toby and Saskia kiss, the arch is raised and they walk under the arch.

Uncle Skipper taps Saskia on the bottom with his cutlass.

Uncle Skipper: Welcome to the navy.

If a dramatic exit appeals to you, then you could release doves or balloons, organise some signwriting or dry ice, throw confetti, blow some wedding bubbles or even have a pyrotechnics display. Releasing butterflies is becoming very popular but needs plenty of lead time—at least six weeks—so that butterflies can be bred. Go to a bridal fair or get on the Net to find out more if any of these ideas appeal to you.

Again, your exit requires some planning. If your ceremony is taking place in the same grounds as your reception, should you organise drinks for your guests while they wait for you to finish your photos? Do you want to stay and meet 'n' greet before off to your favourite, spectacular locations for photos?

Plan. Plan. Plan.

 ## 15. Ceremony booklet

Although not necessary, a ceremony booklet can be a wonderful way of creating a memento of your special day, and it is also a gift for people who couldn't attend. If you haven't got a lot of time, keep it simple and make the booklets yourselves. You can design your booklets in the same colours and style as your invitations, or you can create something unique or new. It can be fun—get a group of friends over and make a night of it. If it is important to you, make sure you are clear about what you want people to do. Enthusiastic family members have been known to veer from the bride and groom's desired look because they think they know better. 'Hello! I don't care if you think that looks daggy. It's my wedding. You can do what you like at yours!'

If you are already doing too much, paper shops and graphic designers, or wedding-stationery companies can assist you. Many advertise their services on the Internet and have online catalogues.

Make sure you work out how the booklets are going to get to the ceremony. Make someone responsible for their safe passage.

Don't give out copies of the full ceremony—at least not until the end of the service! Otherwise your utterings will be obscured by the annoying rustling of paper, and the element of surprise and wonder will be extinguished as people will read along, ahead, and then they are not listening to all the wonderful things that you are saying. After the ceremony, put them in baskets and then assign some of your knee-high-to-a-grasshopper guests to hand them out—they'll love it.

You can include anything you like in the booklet, such as:

* order of ceremony;
* music and procession;
* opening and welcome;

- the blessing;
- readings—what they were and whom they were read by;
- giving away;
- Monitum from the Marriage Act;
- affirmation;
- blessing of the hands;
- vows;
- exchange of rings;
- declaration of marriage;
- signing of register and certificates;
- presentation of marriage certificate;
- a list of thank yous to people for coming and for contributions;
- the names of the wedding party;
- brief description of each attendant's relationship to bride and groom;
- name of the celebrant;
- explanation of any cultural/symbolic acts;
- photos of the wedding party;
- special mention of the people you wish could have been in attendance.

If you would like any further information on the order of ceremony booklets, log on to some of the bridal magazine websites listed in Chapter 11.

 ## 16. Traditions and symbols

In the *Hutchinson Dictionary of Symbols*, Jack Tresidder, says that: 'Traditional symbols form a visual shorthand for ideas . . . some symbols encapsulate the most ancient and fundamental beliefs that humans have had about the cosmos, their place in it' (Tresidder 1997). Symbols and symbolic actions have a great part to play in your marriage service. Mum believes that if your ceremony is devoid of symbolism, you limit people's ability to connect with it.

Rituals or symbolic acts are enmeshed with rites of passage such as weddings. Melbourne civil celebrant Geoffrey Baird believes that rituals are extremely important:

> A lot of words are always spoken in ceremonies and I'm always encouraging people to do things rather than say things. It's not about turning up at a registry office, reading words and reciting stuff—that's one element. I'm always encouraging my clients to look for ways to physicalise the act to make it more powerful. It's all talk, talk, talk. What are you going to *do*?

The prospect of undertaking a symbolic act can be quite daunting as some of us are very shy. But most couples report afterwards that they really loved doing it and they are quite surprised at its lasting power.

Geoffrey Baird had a couple that drew on the tradition of the Chinese hope chest, or glory box, which a woman would bring with her to the marriage ceremony. This couple created their own hope chest and even bought a little old Chinese antique box to use. Geoffrey says the couple passed it around the room and it was blessed by all the guests. 'The chest now sits in the couple's bedroom and they say it is quite amazing in that they can hardly ever walk into their bedroom without seeing it on the shelf. And it reminds them that they are married. It has a power that they didn't quite expect.'

Over the course of human history, every community has developed rituals to symbolise changing states. Many of them can be incorporated into your wedding if you desire. Listed below are some examples of what you could do in your ceremony. It is not a conclusive list nor a detailed analysis of symbolism throughout the ages. There are plenty of books out there which can provide you with more detail. These are just some ideas to get you started.

Unity candle ceremony

The lighting of candles is a universal symbol of unity, and many cultures use candles in rituals. Sydney civil celebrant Nitza Lowenstein uses candles as a way of drawing people from different backgrounds together because they are familiar to most people.

All guests light a candle

Cate and Ashley wanted to use candlelight in their ceremony so they decided to ask every guest to come forward and light a candle which they then placed at the edge of the ceremony space. The result was a profusion of light, laughter and smiles for the couple about to exchange their vows—all accompanied by a love song! Here's what they said:

Celebrant: Cate and Ashley, although as family and friends we cannot prepare you for all that awaits you in your married life together, we can surround you and support you with our love.

Now, would all guests take the opportunity to come forward and light your candle. And as you light your candle you can silently offer your blessings of love and support to Cate and Ashley as they prepare to exchange their vows. While you are lighting your candles, Aidan, Cate's cousin, will sing some love songs.

From Catherine Bearsley

Bride and groom—and their mothers—light a candle

Celebrant: A marriage brings together two individuals, with separate lives, to perform the lifelong pledge of uniting as one. These candles before us symbolise the union of your marriage. The two outer candles represent each of you, as individuals. The centre candle, which you will kindle together, represents the unity, which will continue to develop as you are married. The external candles will remain lit, to show that, even in your unity, you may also remain as individuals.

Mother of bride and mother of groom light candles.

Celebrant: The light of these candles represents the warmth and fragility of love. As you light this single candle from your separate candles, let us reflect on the significance today. Prior to this moment you each walked a separate path. Now, as you light this candle, you embark together on a shared path.

Fiona and Anton light candle.

Celebrant: May the covenant which Fiona and Anton now seal always be blessed with truth and devotion.

From June Newman

Eating and drinking ceremony

Just as the lighting of candles means unity, the drinking of wine and the eating of bread is a universal symbol of sharing and abundance. The drinking of mead, for example, is an integral part of medieval weddings.

Example of wine drinking

When Barbara and Paul married, they drank sake from a bottle sent to them by dear friends who lived in Japan and could not attend their wedding.

Celebrant: Barbara and Paul have chosen this special moment to toast the memory of their very special friends.

Jason pours the sake into the cups.

Celebrant: Barbara and Paul propose the toast to the memory of Yasu Kun and his wife Mi Cha and family who are unable to be here to share this special ceremony with us today.

Barbara and Paul drink a toast together.

From June Newman

Example of bread and wine ceremony

Celebrant: To offer another human being sustenance is to express welcome, care and concern. In the Jewish tradition, to break bread with someone is to show trust, and wine is a symbol of joy, of the richness of life and the sweetness of love. In sharing this food and drink let us be grateful for what we have and wish prosperity for Melanie and Daniel in their lives together.

Celebrant hands Melanie and Daniel a loaf of bread and they tear a piece of bread for the hupah holders, celebrant and themselves. They tear the rest into four large pieces, for each of their parents who then distribute pieces to other guests.

Celebrant: May you eat your fill from the food of the earth. May you never hunger.
Melanie and Daniel: May you never hunger.
The guests reply: May you never hunger.

Everyone eats their piece of bread.

Celebrant hands Melanie the glass of wine. Celebrant and guests also take a glass of wine each.

Celebrant: May you drink your fill from the cup of life. May you never thirst.
Melanie: May you never thirst.
The guests reply: May you never thirst.

Melanie drinks from the glass. Celebrant and the guests also take a sip of wine. Melanie hands the glass back to celebrant.

Celebrant hands the glass to Daniel and says: May you drink your fill from the cup of life. May you never thirst.
Daniel: May you never thirst.
The guests reply: May you never thirst.

From June Newman

Tying the hands

Handfasting, or tying the lover's knot, is an ancient custom in which a man and woman's wrists are bound together to signify that they wish for 'enduring love, fertility and prosperity'—so says Joy Ferguson, the author of *Magickal Weddings* (Ferguson 2001).

Handfasting is becoming a very popular ritual to incorporate in a wedding, and most people use a scarf, decorative cord or ribbon. At the conclusion of the ritual, don't untie the knot! Most people place the ribbon or cord into a special bag or pouch for safekeeping. Some couples even mount the cord after the wedding, to remind them of the vows they have taken. There are many books and websites, such as www.handfasting.com.info, which explain handfasting in detail. The words below form the basis of many handfasting ceremonies.

Example of a handfasting ceremony

Celebrant holds a sash before the bride and groom who grasp each other's left wrist.

Celebrant: Charlotte and Perry have each prepared themselves in their hearts to begin a new life. One built together on a strong foundation of love and respect. This marriage is a rite of passage as the past is left behind as they walk together bound by the ties of love. To symbolise these bonds I hereby bond their left hands together with this cord, which like their love holds them together. I tie a true lover's knot—the hands are tied together and yet they maintain their individuality. May this joining bless your union, with sensitivity and understanding.

The knot is tied and the celebrant strikes the bell three times.

Celebrant: You begin your journey of life shared bound together by the vows of this rite. May the love and passion you share continue to burn in your hearts. May the wind continue to whisper joy into your life. May your union grow with the earth and may your cup of love be ever overflowing (Metrick 1992).

From June Newman

Sand ceremony

When Karen and Lachlan married they wanted to capture part of their wedding and literally bottle it forever! Karen says, 'We have the rings and we have the video, but everyone has rings, and you have to physically take out and play the video. We wanted something really meaningful that we could put on display that would remind us always of our special day.'

Karen and Lachlan devised a sand ceremony as it symbolised their love of the beach and represented them as individuals and as a new couple. After they made their vows, they poured their individual sand into a special vase. Karen says this gesture captured their vows and sealed them in with the sand. 'Now every time we look at the vase, we don't only remember our beautiful wedding but we remember the beautiful words we exchanged as we said our vows on our special day. It makes it that much more special.'

Here's how their sand ceremony was performed:

Celebrant: As a symbol of their marriage today, Karen and Lachlan have chosen to use the sand from Avoca Beach. Just as the Earth and sands have allowed us to look back in time and understand the past, Lachlan and Karen will use this sand today to symbolise their history as two individuals, two separate souls who today will unite and start what will be a history together. As Lachlan and Karen say their vows they seal their promises by pouring their sand into a communal wedding vase. A layer of neutral sand will seal and separate their individual histories and vows.

I now ask Karen and Lachlan's parents to present to them their separate sand cylinders, as a symbol of the love and richness they have provided and which has played such a vital role in the history of these two individuals. We ask that Myra and Les and Dianne and Jim present these cylinders as a blessing to this wedding.

Medieval sword exchange

A sword is swathed in meaning. Throughout history swords have had deep significance—from the legend of Excalibur to the queen using them to dub her knights. Using swords—for peaceful purposes—as a prop in a wedding ceremony can be an extremely dramatic way to emphasise particular parts of the ceremony.

Celebrant takes the sword from the altar and passes it to the best man who passes it to the groomsman who passes it to the groom.

Celebrant: The sword is significant, as it is a symbol of strength, the defender, and a warrior. King Arthur led the crusades with the golden sword, Excalibur.

Roger takes the sword, kneels and offers it to Emily, saying: My most beloved, accept the oath of love which I offer thee. I vow this sword as I vow my body, ever to be at thy service. Like this blade, my heart will be strong. Like this steel my love will endure. Accept it my chosen one. For all which is mine shall now be thine. (Juster-Schofield 2001)

Emily takes the sword in her hands and touches it to her forehead. She returns it to the groom, saying: My most beloved, I accept this oath, sworn on thy blade. Thou knowest what is in my heart as I know what is in thine.

Celebrant: Emily, if thou truly desires to marry this man, I ask thee to take wholeheartedly the blade which is a symbol of strength to him and always be at his service. (Ibid)

Emily kneels, holds the sword up to Roger and says: My most beloved, accept the oath of love which I offer thee. I vow this sword as I vow my soul ever to be at thy service. Like the blade my heart will be strong. Like its value my heart will endure. Accept it my chosen one. For all which is mine will now be thine.

Roger then takes the sword and touches it to his forehead. He returns it to Emily, saying: My most beloved, I accept this oath sworn on this blade. Thou knowest what is in my heart and I knowest what is in thine.

Celebrant: Above thee are the stars. Below thee are the stones. As time does pass remember. Like the stars, should thy love be constant, like a stone should thy love be firm. Be close, yet not too close. Possess one another, yet be understanding. Have patience each with the other for storms will come but they will go quickly. Be free in giving of affection and warmth. Have no fear, and let not the ways or words of the unenlightened give you unease. For the Goddesses and the Gods are with you now and always. (Metrick 1992)

From Trish Juster-Schofield and June Newman

Casting a circle

The use of a circle appears in many religious rituals from all creeds. The circle has had symbolic significance in marriage ceremonies throughout time. A circle symbolises totality, perfection, unity and eternity. It is a symbol of completeness that can include ideas of both permanence and dynamism (Tresidder 1997). Hindu, Jewish and Greek wedding ceremonies all have rituals around circling. Casting a circle is also a central part of Wiccan ceremonies. Many couples choose to cast a circle in their wedding service as a way 'to delineate a space' (Kaldera and Schwartzstein 2004).

When Melanie and Daniel married, they chose a casting the circle ritual as they felt it reflected an important aspect of Melanie's spirituality.

Celebrant casts the circle with dried lavender. As she lights each candle she says: I am casting this circle to create a space that is special for this occasion. Within the circle, we gather together to be here in the moment, leaving aside all distracting thoughts and worries. Use your imagination to help create this safe and joyful space. The circle is as strong as the spirit of those within it.

The circle is created of the five elements that give us life— air, fire, water, earth and spirit. They remind us of the responsibility we have to care for our planet and to tread lightly and respectfully during our time upon it.

Celebrant moves to the spirit altar. She picks up her flint wand, lights the candle and says: The lighting of the spirit candle first, is to give the impression that this candle has always been lit. This symbolically reminds us that spirit cannot be invoked because it is always in and among us. It is all pervasive. We light this candle and take a moment to feel the spirit of this occasion.

Our circle starts in the east—the essence of air. Air is about beginnings, like Daniel's and Melanie's first meeting in Barcelona in 1993. It is new buds in spring, the formation of an idea, a newborn baby's first breath. A yellow candle is a symbol for air. We light it and remember how important air is to our existence.

We move south—the essence of fire. Fire is the will that sparks action, like Melanie and Daniel striving to be together despite the obstacles of geography. It is the passion that follows an idea and the intensity of summer heat. A red candle is a symbol for fire. We light it and remember its ability to hurt and to help, to destroy and to create. Fire commands our respect.

We come to the west—the essence of water. Water is the stamina that sustains us beyond the initial passion and it is this that gives Daniel and Melanie the courage to accept each other's countries as integral to their lives together. Water is the coming of autumn and the tears of endurance. A blue candle is a symbol for water. As we light it, we remember the extent to which we and other species rely on it. The waters of the earth deserve our protection.

And now north—the essence of earth. Earth is the end of a cycle, just as this is the time of a new phase in Melanie and Daniel's partnership—their decision to spend their lives together in marriage. Earth is the slumber of winter, a task completed and the cusp of a new beginning. It is the gentleness that flows from courage and wisdom. A green candle is a symbol for earth. We light it and remember that we all come from the earth and will return to it.

The circle is cast,
we are between the worlds,
beyond the bounds of time,
where night and day,
birth and death,
joy and sorrow
meet as one.

From June Newman, with Melanie and Daniel

Water ceremony

Throughout time water has been an ancient and universal symbol of purity, fertility and the source of life itself (Tresidder 1997, p. 221). Water is part of all cosmologies and can symbolise replenishment and the birth of the new.

Catherine Bearsley devised a unique water ceremony for Cate and Ashley. She says that Cate, whose parents were born in New Zealand, and Ashley, whose family are from Melbourne, wanted to acknowledge their different backgrounds in their marriage ceremony. 'They decided that the universal symbol of water would touch both their life stories, and those of their guests, many of whom had crossed the Tasman from New Zealand for their celebration,' Catherine says.

Cate and Ashley asked their siblings to collect water from significant sources and to present this water in specially chosen jars at the ceremony after the signing of the marriage certificates. Water from each source was then poured into a larger vessel. As another family member read words chosen for the moment, each sibling sprinkled the newly married couple with water. Catherine says, 'It was both a serious and light-hearted moment for the couple, and, as it is with all rituals, surprisingly moving for those who had spent the time preparing for the moment—especially those who collected the water!'

Bringing the waters together (part one)

Celebrant: John and Aoife, Andrew, Renae and Melonie, you have a special task this morning. Water, particularly in Australia, is a powerful, much valued source of life.

Cate, your brother John brings water from Wellington Harbour in New Zealand. New Zealand has been your home—and the home of your parents, grandparents and the generations back that were adventuring settlers from Ireland, Scotland and England.

John pours a little water into the shell held by Liz, the bridesmaid and Cate's sister.

Celebrant: Your brother Andrew brings water from Valley Reserve in Mount Waverley where you grew to adulthood.

Andrew pours a little water into the shell.

Celebrant: Ashley, your sister Renae has brought water from the Murray River, a very important place, where you spent many summers water-skiing.

Renae pours a little water into the shell.

Celebrant: Your sister Melonie has brought water from the Maribyrnong River in Essendon, where you spent much of your childhood.

Melonie pours a little water into the shell.

Celebrant: These waters represent your cultures, ancestors, your family backgrounds and your history. Poured together, they remind us of all the forces of love that come together to make you who you are today.

A blessing with water (part two)

Aoife: Like the waters of the oceans—may your love be a source of life, potential and inspiration.

John sprinkles Cate and Ashley.

Aoife: Like the waters of a river—may your love be limitless, flowing and dynamic.

Andrew sprinkles Cate and Ashley.

Aoife: Like the water that is found in the depths of a well—may your love always rise from your deepest Self.

Renae sprinkles Cate and Ashley.

Aoife: Like the rain that is necessary for life—may your love refresh and revive each other's spirits in difficult times.

Melonie sprinkles Cate and Ashley.

Aoife: With the water from your heritage we bless you and wish for you a life-giving love for all time.

From Catherine Bearsley

Chapter Six
THE POLITICS OF MARRIAGE CEREMONIES

One of the reasons people don't get married is because they are terrified of the familial and friendship conflicts that can arise as a result of making the happy announcement. If you have a complicated, blended family, split along the lines of a political party with various factions not speaking to each other, the prospect of getting married can be far too daunting.

Also, if you're a seasoned parent/sibling/friend pleaser, you're in for a rough trot! If you don't hang on to your dream, you may find yourself living out the cobbled combined dreams of Granny and Mum. 'Now darling, Father Murphy always said that when you grew up he would marry you—wouldn't that be lovely?' GULP.

The time starts now to say 'thank you very much for your idea but this is what I want.' It is difficult though because you might have to decide between how happy you want to be and how much you want to fulfil the dreams of your parents and other family members. Adopt your negotiator's hat. Think about the end point—that you want to be happy at the end of your day, and hopefully many other people will be happy as well. Keep your eye on the prize and what's important. Try not to lose sight of it.

The most popular sites for conflict are: Family. Family. Family. Religion. Religion. Religion.

Here are some of the issues that tend to ignite a few arguments.

Family affairs

If your parents hate the idea of a civil ceremony as they are deeply religious and they want you to marry in a temple or church, you have two options (one may make more people happier than the other):

Option 1—Dig your heels in, say stuff it, and just do what you want

It's your wedding! The problem with just doing what you want is that your parents may never be able to come to terms with it. This option may therefore strain their relationship with you and your lovely for a long time to come and is it worth it? We may like to kid ourselves that we are islands, but we aren't—particularly when we get married. (Remember, if you have kids you are going to need your mum so it's best to keep her on side.) Even though you may hate it, your parents have got expectations about your wedding and marriage—what a bugger! But there are ways to cater to everyone's needs—see below.

Option 2—Give a little

Some couples with deeply religious parents have found a happy compromise by holding a religious ceremony—where just the parents, officials and witnesses are present—before the civil event. This guarantees happy parents which means that you'll be happy even if you wish they didn't have that influence on you. Make them happy and then have the civil renewal of vows a week or a day afterwards. If you do choose this option, all you have to do at the civil service is omit the Monitum, and in your vows and askings use the past tense. You can't pretend that you aren't marrying again; you have already done that in the church or temple.

Alternatively, you can infuse the civil ceremony with elements that are familiar to your religious family. A family priest could bless your union. Readings could come from religious texts. Rituals such as drinking wine, the Jewish ritual of the breaking of the glass, or the Greek exchange of crowns could be easily incorporated into your ceremony.

In times such as these, Upper Hutt civil and religious celebrant Norman Knipe recommends opening up the process to include your parents' opinion. He gives all his clients a pack full of readings and vows and so on for different parts of the marriage ceremony. When problems are encountered with parents, he suggests, if a couple is willing to 'let their parents look through it too. It creates a bridge. And it gives the parents the opportunity to have a little bit of input into the service and they can say, 'wouldn't it be nice to have that . . . and then they can talk.'

Some people may have never attended a civil service so have no idea what to expect. Your parents may be in the same boat. If they can actually see what you are considering, their fears may be allayed.

How do I deal with people that I don't like but that I am related to or obligated to invite?

If you've got your 'me me me me' cap on, ignore them. Exclude them. It's your day, do what you want! However, your wedding day is supposed to be a joyous day, not one blighted by ill feelings. And the wise old owls in our midst would advise that you should be big enough to give those pains minor roles. At least, if Mr or Mrs Unpopular feels included it will contain their influence and can minimise their negative impact. So invite them. And if you have to, let them hand out the booklets, scatter rose petals, ring the bells, usher the people in, and so on. But remember this is a joyous occasion—hopefully one of the happiest days in your life. Open your heart—even if it doesn't want to. Don't exclude, but don't feel that the person in question has to play a major role either. Just let them play a role, however small.

I want my mother, not my father, to walk me down the aisle.

Your dad doesn't have to. Your mum can. Think about the potential fallout though.

Mum and Dad don't talk to each other—what should I do?

Well, don't put them in a dark room alone! Try and minimise their exposure to each other. Lay down the law. 'It's my day. I want you both to come. No funny business between you two in public please. If you feel that you can't do that, then don't come—that's your choice.'

They can sit on the same side, if you're having sides, but of course they don't have to sit next to each other. Put a big strong human barrier between them if necessary. Most people 'pull their heads in' at occasions such as weddings. And it is amazing how nothing may be said but all other family members will move into gear to ensure that there are no scenes.

I don't like my stepmother/stepfather but my father/mother won't come unless she/he is included.

It's a fact of life these days that couples arrive at the wedding ceremony with more than two parents each. Yeah, you may not like her/him, but how much one-on-one time are you going to spend with them anyway? Containment. Practise containment.

In our society today there are more and more blended families. We all bring our pasts with us. It can take years for a family to blend successfully. It's just hard. A wedding is a prime hotspot for all your family's dirty washing to come out.

A marriage ceremony is as political as a Labor Party preselection process. You have to decide what is the most important thing to you—what you can let go and what you want to keep. And on any contentious issue with your ceremony, ask yourself: is it worth it?

When Judy married, she didn't want her stepmother to have a prominent role in the ceremony. But to the outside world, the stepmother had basically raised Judy. Downplaying her role would have led to all sorts of complications which Judy didn't want displayed on her wedding day. 'Getting married is stressful enough without starting World War Three to boot,' says Judy. So even though she didn't want to, Judy made sure that her stepmother had a prominent role in the ceremony. 'My Mum played a part as well. I discussed it with Mum beforehand and we both know the truth and that is what really matters.'

How can I include my children in my ceremony?

There are many ways that you can include your children in your ceremony. For example, you can walk with your child down the aisle, you can issue a certificate welcoming the child into their new family, or make a statement to the child during the ceremony.

Giving a child a bracelet

When Marianne and Dave married they included their small daughter in their ceremony. Marianne says, 'Kim announced herself unexpectedly three days after we made the initial booking and arrangements for the wedding in the Netherlands. We decided to postpone for another year and enjoy the birth of our child first. By this time we had become such a close-knit unit that it felt only natural to include our child and give her our "vows" too.'

In the ceremony, Dave and Marianne exchanged vows and then they each read a poem to each other 'We then stood Kim on top of the table in front of us, read our words to her and gave her a bracelet we had specially made for her, containing a star sapphire which I found in central Queensland the year I met Marianne in 1995', recalls Dave.

Dave: My love for you runs so deep it saturates my heart. But where did it happen? why? and when? and how did it start? Was it when I first glimpsed your beauty?, or on the white sands of Cable Beach?, maybe lying under the desert stars or wading through Tunnel Creek, or driving six weeks through the vast outback where I got to know you inside out, or snorkeling on the Barrier Reef, watching you being chased by a horny coral trout.

But it could have been on Fraser Island bogged up to the door, or was it trekking up Snowdon where I realised I wanted you more? Maybe on Terschelling while cycling through the dunes or camping on an island underneath a Canadian moon? Was it sharing your grief and glory through that epic Visa trip?, or seeing you so stoked surfing as you take off in the lip? The strolls along Plomber as dolphins played in the waves or watching you being attacked by that magpie as we walked around the graves.

So many places, so many times, it's impossible to say just when. Was it yesterday, the day before, was it now or was it then, for what was once two, now is three and whatever happens, good or rough, for how I feel about you, right now, forever isn't long enough. With love.

Marianne: Dave, You're my mate, you're my soulmate, you're my love
You have always been there for me when I needed you most and more
You make me feel free, you let me be myself
When I'm with you life seems light and easy
I love your enthusiasm, your sparkle for life and your sense of adventure.
You are sweet, kind, attentive, patient and gentle
You are the best dad in the world
You complement and inspire me and therefore I want to be with you
I feel we will manage to make our lives fun and stick by our little girl and each other and I hope the day when we have to part will never come . . .
I love you with all my heart.

In Dutch and in English, Marianne and Dave then made a declaration to their daughter Kim and they gave her a bracelet.

Marianne and Dave: Our flesh
Our miracle
Our life
Our everything
Our little girl
We promise
We will always love you
And take care of you
We will always be your friends
And guide you
And as a symbol for all this
We give you this sapphire

Which comes from mother earth
And will ground and protect you
On your journey through life
All our love!!

Giving a child a necklace

When Summer and Liam married, they used the ring ceremony to demonstrate their commitment to Summer's son, Jay.

Celebrant: As a symbol of their union Summer and Liam have chosen to exchange rings. Jay, could you bring the rings? Jay brought the rings to this ceremony as a sign of his happiness that these two people he loves are getting together. Summer and Liam wish to show him, in turn, that they both love and honour him. As a sign of his importance in their family, Summer and Liam wish to give Jay this very special necklace as a visible symbol of their love and the bond the three of them share.

From Marita Wilcox

Using the wedding vows

When Amanda and Michael married, they had a baby son of their own and Amanda had three daughters, aged between eleven and fifteen years, from a previous marriage. They used their wedding vows as a way of incorporating the girls into the ceremony. Celebrant on the day, Clive Rumney, reports that the use of humour in the vows 'was primarily a "bribe" to win the girls' cooperation in what they otherwise thought would have been a "soppy" ceremony.'

Celebrant: Friends, we know that today Michael declares his lifelong commitment to Amanda. But the husband–wife relationship to be established by their marriage will not be the only new relationship created by it. Marriage sets up a whole new network of other relationships, and the most important of these is that which is established between Michael and Amanda's own daughters.

Step relationships can sometimes be difficult for a number of reasons, but with the right attitude they can also be loving and very meaningful. I'm sure that you all know that that attitude is already present in this family, but the important thing is that it now be acknowledged. Michael has requested that this new relationship, and his strong commitment to it, be proclaimed as part of this ceremony. So although it is but a formality, Michael wants now to welcome the girls into this newly created family unit and declare his commitment to them by making some special vows to them.

Michael, do you today promise to do your best to assist Samantha, Annabelle and Olivia in whatever way you can as they grow to adulthood, and to be their guide, mentor and a good father figure to them?

Michael: I do.
Celebrant: And being aware of the important place that you hold in their lives, do you promise to always treat them fairly and with due care and respect?
Michael: I do.
Celebrant: I will now ask the girls for their vows in response. Samantha, Annabelle and Olivia, do each of you promise to be proud of your new family, and to be good and helpful older sisters to your young brother Will, and help him to grow up so that he loves each of you?
Girls: We do.
Celebrant: And do you also promise to do whatever Amanda and Michael tell you to do, to never argue with each other, to always put the phone back, and help with the washing up?
Girls: No!

From Clive Rumney

Using a ribbon ritual

When Robyn and Guido married, it was second time around for both of them and they both had children from their previous marriages. They asked their celebrant, Pat Lane, to devise a ritual that symbolised the beginning of a new family unit. Pat developed a ribbon ritual as it was 'easy for children to manage, looks good and people really like it.'

Celebrant: In days of old, Celtic marriage ceremonies used coloured ribbons and these were used in a myriad of ways. Today, I hold seven coloured ribbons and will ask Guido and Robyn's children and respective mothers, one at a time, to come forward and take a ribbon and present it to Guido and Robyn so that the ribbon, with its unique significance, can be a reminder of the elements and the messages symbolised by the colours.

The children each present their ribbons, kiss Guido and Robyn and return to their position in the bridal party.

Nathan—presents a green ribbon, symbolising 'earth'. Guido and Robyn, this ribbon will remind you that you are partners in life and love and because of this, you will work together always for the best.

   Matt—presents a yellow ribbon symbolising 'air'. Guido and Robyn, this ribbon will remind you to promise each other to communicate as clearly as you can with each other and to share your thoughts, share your hopes and dreams, as well as your fears and insecurities.

   Amelia—presents a red ribbon, symbolising 'fire'. Guido and Robyn, this ribbon represents the power and passion in your relationship and will remind you both never to take each other for granted and to share yourselves totally with each other.

   Alecia—presents a blue ribbon symbolising 'water'. Guido and Robyn, this ribbon represents emotion and love. This ribbon will remind you both that you must always put each other first in life, considering the feelings of each other in all your decisions.

   Leah—presents a pink ribbon symbolising 'romance'. Guido and Robyn, this ribbon will remind you to keep romance alive in your relationship, enduring love that has warmth, power and endurance. Romance needs to be created and it is mostly about the little things, ways to make your partner's day a bit more special—little surprises: a special note, a romantic card, a special 'toast' with a glass of wine, a flower, a chocolate and sharing 'some fun'.

A family is the social unit that grows from the love of a man and a woman. With time and circumstance we can belong to more than one. A family is not measured by the mansion on the hill, or the house at the beach, but the people within. We are born into them and grow into others in our hearts. It is a place where we experience love and joy, warmth and laughter. It is acceptance of weakness and support of endeavour.

Today, Guido and Robyn, your respective mothers also wish to symbolise their thoughts to you by presenting ribbons.

Mothers come forward, each present their ribbons and return to their respective places.

Beverley Eames—presents a purple ribbon, symbolising 'insight and companionship'. True friendship provides so many of the essentials for a happy life. This companionship is the mortar which will bond you together in harmony, and it is the calm, warm protection you will need when the world outside seems cold and chaotic. This ribbon will also remind you that your families are committed to supporting you in your endeavours.

Lelia Cossignani—presents a white ribbon symbolising 'spirit'. This ribbon will remind you both that everything in life is a circle, which has no beginning and no end but all things, like the seasons, keep returning. You need to both take responsibility for your own capacity to bring joy into the family unit and your marriage.

These ribbons are a symbol of your love and commitment to each other. The challenge is to be able to pick up the loose ends that occur. This relationship between Guido and Robyn is woven with a rich tapestry of lifetime choices and experiences. And in this lifetime, the combined forces of love and respect will guide this new relationship into the future; never demanding, or taking from each other, but giving without measure, continuing to build a life, sharing all joy and sadness together.

Somehow, out of all the twists and turns their lives have taken, Guido and Robyn have found each other. It almost seems as though they were given a 'meant to be' moment to meet again, to get to know one another and to now embrace their destiny together. And 'love' will make this happen. Amelia will now read a verse dedicated to Guido and Robyn.

Amelia: If you can love one another through the sunshine and the storm
And keep the flame of true devotion glowing bright and warm,
If you can give each other room to grow and change and learn,
Yet still hold one another close in mutual concern,
If you can be both lovers and the very best of friends,
And face together hand in hand the challenges life sends
If you can offer patience, comfort and real understanding,
Encourage one another's efforts, yet be understanding,
If you can show true love and faith in everything you do,
Then married life will surely hold much joy for both of you.

From Pat Lane

Difficult children

If your children are not keen, or are resentful, about you marrying— good luck! You may have moved on but your children haven't. They may still want you to marry your ex, and your wedding may not be the most joyous moment in their lives. If they are adamant that they don't want to be involved, don't try to swim against the tide and make them do something that they don't want to. It will only end in disaster.

Or you could try a gesture from you to them—but kids can be a tough audience. You could make a public statement to them; do a symbolic act such as planting a tree to signify a new life, or bribe them with something that they have always wanted . . .

Hilary Smith from Relationship Services Whakawhanaungatanga advises that you don't leave it to the wedding to deal with children who are hostile to the idea of you walking down the aisle again. She says that the age of your children may impact on how you deal with the problem. 'Children who are still dependent on parents may need some counselling to help them deal with their feelings about the end of their parents' relationship and how they adjust to a new relationship for one of their parents. They need to know that they will still get what they need from their parent. So you probably need counselling for them, and counselling for you all together.'

The idea of a parent re-marrying can also hit adult children hard. Hilary recommends: 'honest conversation, listening to their feelings and accepting them. Don't expect them to be happy just because you are.' *

My parents are paying for my wedding and they want to dictate what kind of ceremony we have.

Theoretically, it has nothing to do with them. But some couples do encounter this attitude. You don't get something for nothing! Establish what it is exactly that your parents want and work out what you think is open for negotiation. Mum wants Uncle Arthur to do a reading? Have three readings rather than two. Dad wants a religious service with the Archbishop and you're an atheist? Mmmmm. Call the UN?

Hilary Smith from Relationship Services Whakawhanaungatanga, asks: 'If the marriage is your public statement about your relationship, what statement are you making if someone else decides how it will be?' As for how to deal with parents who insist on having a say in the wedding as they are paying for it, Hilary says that:

> A couple needs to establish some boundaries about how much direct influence their families have on the relationship and a wedding is one place to do this. You don't need to be hurtful or rejecting, just be clear that you are grateful for any assistance, but it is your wedding. You might try describing the service you want and the specific help or support you would like from them. Ask if they would be willing to help in those ways.

So if the money is going to compromise good family relationships and stop you from having a wedding that expresses what *you* want to say about your relationship, then you don't need to accept it.

---

* A wonderful book that may help you through this particularly rocky path, is, *Stepfamily Life: why it is different—and how to make it work* by Margaret Newman.

We've had a registry office wedding and now we would like another ceremony. Do we need a celebrant?

No. You've done the legal deed. You can only have one lawful marriage ceremony with the same partner. However, you can re-commit and renew your vows as many times as you like—as Sarah and Tommy did below.

Renewal of vows ceremony

There are a number of reasons why a couple may choose to have a reaffirmation of vows ceremony. Tommy, from Denmark, and Australian-born Sarah married at the Town Hall in Venice and wanted another ceremony in Australia with all of Sarah's family and friends, a few months later.

In this ceremony, they reaffirmed their askings, made personalised vows to each other, exchanged rings and signed what they called a 'commitment certificate', which was also signed by every guest as a symbol of their loving support of their relationship.

Celebrant: Today is so very special; it is a beautiful and joyous occasion because it is a celebration of Sarah and Tommy's marriage which took place on 10 August 2000, at the Town Hall in Venice.

Sarah's parents, Judy and Ralf, welcome Tommy into the Simpson family and wish me to declare their loving support for this union and their promise that they will do everything in their power to help it last a lifetime.

Sarah and Tommy are providing us with a unique opportunity today to publicly support them and their union, with this gathering of their family, friends and community in Australia, as they reaffirm in front of us, the commitments that they have already made to each other, to spend their lives together in marriage.

The celebrant then went into some depth about the history of their relationship as Sarah and Tommy wanted their Australian

*family and friends to know Tommy's background and
something about how they met and came to love each other.*

Reading One—'We Two' by Kuan Tao-Sheng

The asking

*This was done in the past tense as Tommy and Sarah had
already made pledges to each other in their marriage ceremony.*

Celebrant to Tommy: Tommy, you have taken Sarah to be your
lawful wedded wife?

Will you love, comfort and respect her, be honest with her
and stand by her through whatever may come, so you can
genuinely share your life together?

Tommy: I will.

Celebrant to Sarah: Sarah, you have taken Tommy to be your
lawful wedded husband?

Will you love, comfort and respect him, be honest with him,
and stand by him through whatever may come, so you can
genuinely share your life together?

Sarah: I will.

Vows

*In Venice, they made standard vows to each other so they took
the opportunity with this ceremony to write personalised vows.*

Celebrant: Sarah and Tommy are about to take their vows in
our presence, please everyone be still and listen to what they
are saying to each other, so that if they ever encounter difficult
times we, as their community, can remind them of the solemn
promises they have made to each other today.

Sarah and Tommy together say: We pledge to one another to:
- Love each other for eternity.
- Always communicate.
- Always care for, support and protect each other and our family.
- Continue to live our fairytale.
- Continuously make our voyage in this life and beyond,
  adventurous.

- Enjoy life and live it to the fullest.
- Grow old together satisfied knowing we have accomplished our goals in life.

Celebrant to Sarah and Tommy: Do you both promise to never forget how you feel today and promise to make it easy for each other to remember.
Sarah and Tommy: We do.

Exchange of rings

Celebrant explains: In Nordic countries the engagement ring is the most important ring, a gold band is given at the engagement. Both receive the rings as a sign of commitment and to show others of their involvement with each other.

A ring historically represents eternity, unity, wholeness and commitment. The circular symbolism of the ring makes it an emblem of completion, strength and protection, as well as continuity.

It is only when the female is married that she receives a second ring.

Sarah and Tommy sign the commitment certificate.
The celebrant then presents the certificate to Sarah and Tommy and says the following.

Celebrant: Everyone here today has signed this certificate so Tommy and Sarah can take it with them to remind them of the support and love of the Simpson family and everyone that was here for them today in Australia.

Celebrant asks everyone to toast Sarah and Tommy and join hands in applause.

Celebrant: Be always reassured of the support and love that all gathered here have for you both and your marriage.

Let's celebrate this great day!

From June Newman

How to blend different religious or cultural traditions

The other area of controversy is religion. Just because you are having a civil ceremony does not mean you have to exclude who you are. Whatever your cultural or religious background, elements from your tradition can be included in your ceremony. Even though you may not have been a practising member of your church or an active member of your community for some years, it is amazing how, once you make the decision to marry, your history suddenly becomes important.

You can take various aspects of different cultures and weave them into your ceremony quite easily. Out in the big wide world, you will find celebrants who specialise in these types of ceremonies. You will also find many celebrants willing to do the research with you to create a ceremony which you feel reflects your religious traditions or cultural practices.

Can I include anything that I want?

Yes. There are no restrictions to the civil service. But, if you are going to incorporate a religious custom into your marriage ceremony make sure you do it correctly or you may risk offending some of your guests. Sydney civil celebrant Nitza Lowenstein advises that when you drink wine and break a glass at a Jewish wedding, for example, you do not drink from and break the same glass, as it is very bad luck. Be careful!

How do I go about it?

Get down to the library—there are so many books on the subject. Start surfing the Net. Talk to members of your community. It's study time. Read up on the marriage rituals associated with your religion or cultural background and talk with your lovely. What's important to him or her? To you? Your family? Can everyone's wishes be accommodated? Some civil celebrants specialise in cross-cultural ceremonies. Members of your community will know some good contacts.

Some cultural and religious wedding traditions

At the outset, let's just say we are going to sweep with a very broad brush here. It is impossible to attempt to sum up the marriage practices of some of the largest and oldest religions and cultural groups on earth in the scope of this book. We have not covered all cultures or religions. All we seek to do is alert you to some popular practices and beseech you to go and find out more information. Talk to members of your community; go to the library; talk to your favourite priest, holy man or woman—and please don't quote us to anyone who looks like a religious scholar or cross-cultural expert!

Catholic

The Catholic marriage has a number of features that can be incorporated into an inter-faith or civil marriage ceremony. A typical order of service for a Catholic marriage celebration, as outlined in *Together for Life* by Joseph M. Champlin, includes readings from the Old and New Testament of the Bible, responsorial psalms, Gospel acclamation and verse, the exchange of rings and vows, nuptial blessings and a candle ceremony. The marriage rite typically concludes with reciting the *Lord's Prayer* and a final blessing.

If you want to include elements of a Catholic service in your wedding, then consider including the *Lord's Prayer* or passages from the Bible such as: *They Are No Longer Two, But One Flesh*. Mark 10:6–9 (ESV):

A reading from the Holy Gospel according to Mark
Jesus said:
'From the beginning of creation,
God made them male and female.
For this reason a man shall leave his mother and father
And be joined to his wife
And the two shall become one flesh.
So they are no longer two but one flesh.
Therefore what God has joined together,
No human being must separate.'

You could also include a prayer for both of you as a couple which you recite together. For example:

We ask, finally, that in our old age we may love one another as deeply and cherish each other as much as we do at this very moment. May you grant these wishes which we offer through your Son, Jesus Christ, our Lord (Champlin 2002).

Anglican

An Anglican service follows a similar path to that of a Catholic wedding. After the bride arrives, there are readings with at least one from the Bible, followed by a sermon. The couple then declares their intention to marry, makes their declarations of love and vows, exchanges rings, recites prayers, and then registers the marriage.

The Church of England's website at www.cofe.anglican.org has a colossal bounty of material for Church of England weddings. For example, the site has a suggestion for a pastoral reading before the marriage ceremony commences, which starts with the following words: 'A wedding is one of life's great moments, a time of solemn commitment as well as good wishes, feasting and joy. St John tells us how Jesus shared in such an occasion at Cana, and gave there a sign of new beginnings as he turned water into wine' (Archbishop's Council 2000). It concludes with a reading from a letter from St Paul to the Corinthians.

Jewish

There are many aspects to a Jewish wedding ceremony; from the Ketubah; to the bride circling the bridegroom; to the breaking of the glass at the conclusion of the ceremony. Here are a few customs you may want to include or adapt for your wedding ceremony.

The Huppah

A huppah is a canopy held up by four poles, under which a Jewish marriage ceremony takes place. It symbolises the couple's new home. Joan Hawkhurst in her book, *Interfaith Wedding Ceremonies*, says that 'the flimsiness of the huppah is a reminder that the only thing that is real about the home is the people in it who love and choose to be together—to be a family. The only anchor that they will have will be holding on to each other's hand. The huppah is the house of promises. It is the home of hope' (Hawkhurst 1997).

Blessing over the wine

The blessing over the wine is known as the Kiddush and is part of most Jewish celebrations and holidays (Lerner 1999). In a marriage service, the blessing over the wine is usually recited once before you exchange your rings and vows and once as part of the seven traditional blessings. It involves the couple drinking from a silver goblet while a prayer is recited.

Breaking of the Glass

Just as church bells are rung at the end of a Christian marriage, people of the Jewish faith smash a wine glass. A glass goblet is wrapped in a piece of cloth and placed at the foot of the groom who then proceeds to step on it, shattering the glass (Brownstein 2002). One explanation for this custom is that the loud noise of both church bells and breaking glass scares away the evil spirits wishing harm to the newly married couple (Hawkhurst 1997). If you decide to do this as well as the blessing over the wine, make sure you use two different glasses.

Greek

There are a number of elements to the beautiful and ritualised Greek or Eastern Orthodox wedding ceremony.

'After the couple have been betrothed and have exchanged rings, for example, they are crowned with "crowns of glory and honour" which signify the establishment of a new family under God' (Fitzgerald 2004).

The crowns, which are white and made of metal, are joined by a ribbon and establish the couple as king and queen of their home. Near the end of the service, the couple drink from a common cup which is reminiscent of the wedding of Cana. It symbolises how they will share the burdens and the joy of their new life together.

In many civil ceremonies, couples of Greek origin choose to incorporate a crossing the stefana (crowns) into their ceremony.

When Fiona and Anton married, their best man stepped behind the bride and groom and interchanged the crown three times as a witness to a sealing of their union.

Hindu

There is no, one Hindu wedding ceremony that is practised throughout the global Hindu community. Some of the following rites and rituals are part of a standardised Hindu service in the United States, and some of them appear in ceremonies in Australia and New Zealand. Do a search on the Net for Vedic marriage ceremony and you will be hit with an explosion of material. A Vedic marriage ceremony can include the following:

- Raksha bandhan—cords are tied to the wrists of both the bride and groom.
- Garlanding—the bride and groom exchange garlands made of flowers. This expresses the desire of the bride and groom to marry.
- Homam—in the centre of the wedding altar, a fire is kindled. Fire represents a witness.
- Sapta Padi—in South India the couple walk seven steps together to signify their friendship and in the north, each round is a specific blessing (Bose 2004).

Vietnamese

Myly Nguyen, a Melbourne civil celebrant, performs many marriages for members of the Vietnamese community. She says Vietnamese weddings typically take place in the bride's home at a time that has been determined by a fortune teller.

On the day of the wedding, the groom's family go to the bride's home and bring a set of traditional gifts in red boxes, wrapped in red paper, for the bride's family. Each red box contains jewellery— wedding ring and band, jade bangle, necklace and earrings—as well as wine, cake and four to six different kinds of foods that represent happiness, longevity, good luck, etc.

The women wear an Ao Dai (long dress). And the men could be in suits or a male traditional Ao Dai. The groom's family enter the bride's house usually led by an old couple that are the most healthy and successful among the relatives. This represents a wish that the to-be-wed couple will have a blessed life together.

The civil marriage celebrant, sometimes a respected person among the bride's relatives, welcomes the guests and asks the bride's parents to present their daugher. This part of the ceremony is similar to the 'Giving Away' in a western wedding ceremony.

The ceremony starts in front of the altar. First the bridal couple kneel down and pray, asking their ancestors' permission to be married. They then ask for a blessing for their family-to-be.

A candle ceremony occurs next, symbolising the joining of the bride and goom and their families. The candles are usually lit by the fathers of the bride and groom.

The celebrant then reads the Monitum from the Marriage Act and does the askings. The groom's mother then opens one of the red boxes and puts all the jewellery on the bride and the couple exchange their vows and wedding rings. The declaration of marriage is made and the official wedding certificates are signed in front of both families and relatives.

After the presentation of the wedding certificate, the couple then turns around and bows to both parents to say thank you. The couple's parents will then take turns to give their blessing and give the newly-weds valuable gifts such as money. The couple returns to the groom's house where they are greeted by relatives, friends and well-wishers.

Some stories from the frontline

Gail and Paul

Gail and Paul's wedding ceremony was complicated by the fact that Paul is Jewish and Gail is not. 'We had to do this intense negotiation,' Gail says. 'We couldn't have the wedding on a Saturday, as that would have horrified Paul's Jewish family and I didn't particularly want it on a Sunday so we had it on a Wednesday.'

However, because they didn't want a religious ceremony, they chose a celebrant and kept it 'fairly simple'. Gail says, 'We did a reading from the Old Testament. That went down well with the Jews and the Christians! Offended no one there. It took a lot of finding. It was pretty good. And we wrapped up and smashed a glass, which made Paul's Mum happy!'

Ella and Vikram

When Vikram and Ella decided to get married, they wanted to make sure that both of their cultural and religious traditions were evident in their marriage ceremony. Although not particularly religious, Vikram knew that a Hindu ceremony would be important to his family. Ella, who had been brought up as a Catholic, says, at that time, her family were more flexible about letting go of traditions. 'We could have gone to our local Catholic church but Vikram and his family would have found that very weird. We wanted somebody that we liked and we had to keep our families happy. We had already met with two celebrants whom we hadn't liked, then Vikram's family said they knew a Hindu priest who was also a civil celebrant.'

With the blessings of both families, Ella and Vikram met with the celebrant and knew immediately that he was the one. Ella says, 'He was hilarious. He was really sweet and funny. He was really inclusive. And I think that's the thing you have to be conscious of, if you are going to cross cultures, you want everyone to feel a part of it.'

With the help of their celebrant, who explained the various elements of a Hindu wedding service and was 'a wealth of ideas', they created a ceremony that blended parts of both traditions together. Held upstairs at the Bondi Beach Pavilion, on the hottest December day in 40 years the ceremony included many ingenious adaptations.

For example, in Hindu tradition, the ceremony should occur in a 'mendip' (a canopy), but 'we couldn't have that so we had an altar and an Indian umbrella with elephants printed on it and it was decorated with garlands of flowers'. Ella also says her arrival was 'more western style', with her father giving her away. 'Dad had to say something about Dharma, and he got it wrong but it didn't matter. I just wanted to make sure that I was respectful to Dad and included him in the service.' Ella also adds that some of the Indian guests found her arrival quite odd 'because at an Indian wedding the groom normally arrives at the ceremony on a white horse—it's all about the groom arriving and not the bride!'

For the vow part of the ceremony, they adapted the Hindu seven-step ceremony. 'We made them much simpler and put them into English. We took a step together for each idea.' The ceremony also included huge garlands of fresh flowers that were placed on the bride and groom and a 'tying together' with a special piece of ribbon.

'In the end,' Ella says, 'it was funny how all the non-Indians were saying, "oh it's so different" and the Indians were saying "oh it's so different" so it was different for everybody. We had a great time. Before you get married you think the ceremony should be kind of serious and you might cry, but we really enjoyed all of ours because the celebrant was likable, funny and had everyone laughing. It was really joyous'.

Militza and Nico

Canberra celebrant Peter Hyland developed a ceremony with a couple who had an Eastern Orthodox background in conjunction with their relatives and representatives from their local Church. Here's an outline of the ceremony:

The celebrant invited Nico's sister, Mary, to explain the Eastern Orthodox Sacrament of Marriage.

Mary: First the rings are exchanged three times to create interdependence upon each other, signifying an everlasting relationship.

Candles are then presented to symbolise the purity of their lives, which will shine with the light of virtue.

Following this the Kumbada, or best man, will crown Nico and Militza. When the crowns are placed on their heads they become the King and Queen of their home, founders of a new generation which they will rule with wisdom, justice and integrity.

Drinking from the common cup signifies that from this moment on they will share everything in life, their joys will be doubled and their sorrows halved.

Kumbada leads Nico and Militza around the table three times anti-clockwise—holding onto the ribbon between the stefanas.

Nico and Militza then take their first steps as a married couple. Circling around the table symbolises a perfect orbit around the centre of life, an eternity of love.

Finally the Kumbada removes the crowns with a blessing sealing their marriage.

CHAPTER SEVEN
CHOOSING THE SURPRISE CARD

There are a lot of reasons why people choose a surprise wedding. For some, a surprise wedding means that the couple can, in a way, exercise more control over their big day and keep a lid on costs. For others, springing a wedding on their friends is a way of inflicting a delicious surprise on folks, especially if they're convinced that the couple who has been living together for years is never going to tie the knot.

Veteran of a number of surprise weddings and Melbourne celebrant Marita Wilcox recommends that if clients are thinking of organising a surprise wedding, 'they should organise it to coincide with another celebration—a birthday, anniversary, engagement, Christmas, Easter, naming, retirement, housewarming, bon voyage and so on'. A brilliant idea, this prepares the guests for a special occasion so no one arrives in their stubbies and thongs but it means that the focus is off the bride and groom (for the time being at least).

When Fiona and Anton married, they didn't want all the 'dramarama' that can come after making the announcement to their nearest and dearest. Fiona says, 'We wanted to get married but we didn't want any fuss, or something that was too expensive. We wanted it to be about us. The more we spoke about it, the more we realised that a surprise wedding was the way to go.'

So they gathered all of their family and friends to a hall under the guise of their engagement party. 'About two hours into the party, Anton and I disappeared and got changed into our wedding outfits. Anton got up on stage and said, "Has anyone seen Fiona?" and then the deejay played a song by Elvis and my Dad and I appeared. Everyone parted as we made our way up to the stage and the celebrant announced that the marriage was going to begin. A lot of people were surprised. Some initially weren't too impressed but in the end everyone was fine about it.'

A word of warning—if you're thinking of having a surprise wedding, Marita recommends you should think carefully about who you should tell. 'I did one surprise wedding where the elderly (92-plus) grandmother became very, very distressed and upset with the surprise and the grooms' parents were cross that they were not told and at the state it put the grandmother in. Both sets of parents were hurt that the witnesses knew but no one from the family did. It all worked out but there were undercurrents of peevishness!'

A word of warning if you are intending to surprise your partner with a marriage ceremony—you can't spring it on him or her as he or she is legally obliged to sign a Notice of Intention to Marry form at least one month and a day before the ceremony.

To make a surprise wedding work you need to prepare. You need to discuss, in detail, with your celebrant the hows, wheres and whens and who is going to be involved. At least two trusted people should know about it so they can help it work. Make sure you tell anyone who is elderly, infirm or has high blood pressure, as you don't want the excitement to cause them discomfort. Finally, if you're going to pull off a surprise successfully, you must have a rehearsal to make sure that all the pieces fall into place seamlessly.

How some other couples have done it . . .

The following ceremonies were all conducted by Melbourne wonder-celebrant Marita Wilcox.

40th birthday party with wedding ceremony

The occasion was a casual afternoon/evening barbecue to celebrate Tony's 40th birthday, and families, children and friends had gathered. Lynelle and Tony had been together for twelve years and had two children as well as Lynelle's child from a previous marriage. Only a few of the 60 guests knew about the wedding—Lynelle's elderly grandmother, mother and brother, the couple's children and Tony's brother. The celebrant, Marita, mixed amongst the guests as a friend of Lynelle's mother.

Marita says that Tony gave a short, funny, yet emotional and serious speech about life, friends and love, then announced that Lynelle was pregnant again and joked that the only thing left to do was to marry her. 'Everyone laughed,' Marita says, 'as this was known to all to be on the couple's "no no never" list!'

'Tony hushed the guests, then, seriously, asked Lynelle to marry him. She accepted and everyone cheered and clapped. Tony then said "Well let's do it now!" and there was much laughter until he called for a celebrant and I put my hand up and came forward. The guests were dumbfounded, cheering, crying, totally amazed!'

Celebrant: Hello everyone! My name is Marita Wilcox and I have never met Lynelle's mother before in my life! And, yes, I am a civil marriage celebrant and I am here today to join together in marriage Lynelle and Tony. They thank you all for coming, especially those who travelled from far and wide to be here today. Tony and Lynelle really appreciate that you are able to spend this, their special occasion, with them.

As you all know, Tony and Lynelle love and trust each other and have a very special bond through their beautiful children . . . in other words, they are living in sin. They have now seen the error of their ways and have chosen to commit themselves through this simple yet very meaningful ceremony to further strengthen the special bond that they already share. This is not their first marriage, but it is the first time that they are getting married to each other . . .

Engagement party at a restaurant with wedding ceremony

Friends and family of Ange and Jack gathered at a restaurant for their engagement party. Only the two witnesses knew about the wedding. During the speeches Jack started telling everyone some 'personal adventure stories' which gave Ange an excuse to shriek with embarrassment and run out of the room.

Marita says the guests all laughed, thinking it was a joke, then Jack talked of his love for Ange. 'He said he couldn't wait to be married and thought he may as well do it now. He called for a celebrant and I came forward. The music started and Ange, who had changed into her wedding dress, which had been her mother's, made a stunning re-entrance to an absolutely amazed but thrilled audience.'

Celebrant: Welcome everyone to this wonderful occasion. It is an absolute pleasure to conduct this ceremony for Ange and Jack whose relationship has blossomed over the years that I have known them.

Let it not be thought that two independent spirits cannot meet in trust, in partnership and in love. For here are two whose paths have crossed, each path an adventure in itself; who now, together in love, go on in exploration and adventure unending, confined not by doctrine, creed or prejudice, humbled only by the generosity, forgiveness and kindness of one to another.

Today's ceremony is to celebrate Jack and Ange's commitment to each other.

For them, this is more than a ritual in which they wish to share with all of you their expressions of love for each other. Today will mark the point in their relationship that brings together the past, the present and the future. It is also an opportunity to bring together everyone they love to witness this moment.

Naming ceremony followed by marriage ceremony

When Marcia and Evan married, they wanted a very brief ceremony. They had been together for about twelve years and had often declared their firm intention never to marry. They gathered all their friends together to celebrate the naming of their son, Harvey. There was a very relaxed and casual atmosphere, with lots of children. Even though all the players looked casual, they had rehearsed their parts.

The naming ceremony was performed by Marita, who was of course also the celebrant.

Celebrant: Evan and Marcia have invited you to take part in this ceremony as you are the people who have played a part in their lives, and who they wish to play a part in Harvey's life. They thank you for your love and support. So let us share the joy of this occasion and name this child. Harvey James Watts, may life's richest joys and blessings be yours. May you grow in body and mind to adulthood in a loving and peaceful world. May you bring joy to your parents, your family and friends. We wish you long life and happiness on this, your Name Giving Day.

To Harvey!

The naming ceremony concluded with music, 'Beautiful Boy' by John Lennon, and after about five minutes of congratulations and so on, Marcia and Evan went back to the microphone under the guise of Marcia 'wanting to say a few words about family'. This led to Evan asking 'So why don't we make it legal Marce?' and ultimately, after much good-natured taunting and laughter, to Marcia declaring 'Everyone welcome to our wedding!'

Celebrant: Welcome again! This is for real! This marriage is the result of many a discussion between Marcia and Evan and they have come to the conclusion that they want a public declaration of their union. For Marcia and Evan, this ceremony marks the confidence they feel in their enduring friendship and is an expression of the closeness between them, a closeness intensified by the birth of their vibrant, happy son, Harvey.

Marcia and Evan's love is not about being totally absorbed in each other but looking outward in the same direction. And I quote them: 'While we give ourselves in love, we do not give ourselves away . . .'

Chapter Eight
HOW TO ELOPE

Now some people just get sick of the wedding fiasco and think bugger it—we're off to Europe. Others have always dreamed of eloping and escaping to a deserted island and marrying in bare feet, the bride in a beautiful, sheer white dress, holding a pineapple, the groom damp from a morning swim. As with anything, eloping has pros and cons. Some couples have had gorgeous romantic ceremonies that were as perfect as they had always dreamed. Others have eloped and come back to family members so angry that they haven't spoken to each other for months and even years afterwards.

Consider this, if you want to elope, and then have a party immediately afterwards, why can't you just include your nearest and dearest or just your parents in your wedding? When Kylie's mother found out that Kylie was eloping the next day, she was devastated. Her mother had always dreamed of seeing her daughter in her wedding dress. Kylie says, 'I had no idea that it would mean so much to Mum. It never even crossed my mind.'

This story is not a fable to stop you from eloping but you should think about the possible repercussions. Eloping can highlight how difficult the whole process of getting married is—the delicate balance between what you want and what your loved ones want.

In the pro corner, eloping allows you to:

Have the ceremony exactly the way you want it

You have complete creative control of the whole wedding shebang. You can live your dream—get married in the USS *Enterprise* in Vegas or fly down to Antarctica.

Save money

Even if you are having an elaborate holiday and getting married, paying for just the two of you can be significantly cheaper than feeding and watering your circle of family and friends.

Avoid family quagmires

Getting married in your family may be downright terrifying as it may present many opportunities for old family battles to be ignited. Eloping can mean you avoid all that.

In the con corner, eloping may mean:

Potential high miff factor

Try as they might to understand, your parents, close relatives or guardians have all been dreaming about your wedding day since you were tiny, and eloping takes their dream away from them. (Even though this can be the very thing that makes it so damn attractive . . .)

Possible diminished sense of occasion

It may be difficult to create a sense of significance in what you are doing if your entire wedding consists of just the bride and groom and two witnesses. Of course, that may be just the way you like it.

You miss out on the collective joy of your circle

Even though it can be a rough road making it to the Big Day, when the day itself dawns you will be overwhelmed by how you are surrounded by love, hope and goodwill—all day. Celebrants report that it is only the die-hardest-nastiest-ninnies that let their ill will surface on a wedding day, and, thankfully, they are extremely rare. Everybody else loves weddings. Your family and friends will be so pleased to be there and they will shower you with their love. If you elope, you can miss out on that.

Don't do it if:

- You really care about what your parents or other people who are important to you think. The guilt could drive you, and your partner, crazy as you will go on and on about it, and it may stain your memory of your wedding day.
- You can't keep a secret. The whole point of eloping is that it is a secret. If you tell people then it could all get very messy, again spoiling a day that is supposed to be the foundation for a wonderful life together.
- You have just made the decision to elope, and it's dark outside and the clock says 3 a.m. Go back to bed. Sleep. See how you feel in the morning!

If you decide to do it:

- Start the process and look for the right place and celebrant.
- Seek a celebrant or a marriage coordinator who will go the extra mile—who'll bring along champagne or allow you to get ready in their homes, or whatever else you require. Emily and Roger decided to elope because they didn't want the expense of a full ceremony and were thrilled when the celebrant arrived with a table, beautiful tablecloth, some champagne, glasses and a miniature wedding cake.
- Start researching. Of course there are lots of books devoted to this topic. There is the comprehensive *Let's Elope: The Definitive*

Guide to Eloping, Destination Weddings and Other Creative Wedding Options by Lynn Beahan and Scott Shaw, and *Beyond Vegas: 25 Exotic Wedding and Elopement Destinations Around the World* by Lisa Tabb and Sam Silverstein.

And there are many companies that will help you organise a local or international elopement. For example, in Noosa Heads on Queensland's gorgeous Sunshine Coast, a company called The Noosa Wedding Ring will organise your entire wedding for around A$2000.

Dealing with the aftershock

One way to appease disappointed relatives is to organise a renewal of vows ceremony/party upon your return. Or you could include those closest family members who you know would be deeply upset if they couldn't participate.

Eloping overseas

For Australian couple Kerrie and David, eloping seemed the right thing to do. 'We'd been together a long time,' David says, 'and our families were always pressuring us, "When are you getting married? When are you getting married?" Kerrie wasn't the white-wedding kind of girl so when I proposed, and she agreed, we knew that we wanted to do something different. We hadn't told anyone, and we already planned to travel, so we thought why not combine the two?'

Kerrie says, 'There weren't any issues with our families. It was just something that we wanted to do. We felt that whatever we wanted to do, they would be happy with and they were.'

David and Kerrie started calling embassies and consulates in Europe to find a suitable place for their marriage. After a lot of phone calls, they chose to get married in Austria. David says, 'It was practicality really. In some places like Ireland you had to stay as a resident for six weeks in one county and if no one objects then you can get married. We were away for only three months so time was an issue. So we decided on Vienna—you only needed to be there for three days. Everyone who gets married there has to do it in a registry office with a civil ceremony before they have a church ceremony.'

It took a lot of planning and organising, David says, made especially difficult because neither of them spoke German. 'Everything had to be in German,' David says, 'and we had to get our parents' marriage certificates which was tricky and we had to put money into a bank account.'

But as soon as they arrived in Vienna they knew they had made the right decision. Kerrie says, 'We struck it lucky. It was unbelievable, fantastic, perfect.' Even the registry office was gorgeous. It had an exhibition of contemporary art. The building was beautiful.'

On the morning of their wedding, they posted some letters and bought a bouquet of roses. They changed in their hotel room and took a taxi, 'a Mercedes with a sunroof and a driver dressed in a tie— a normal cab for Vienna!', to the registry office.

The service at the registry office lasted about 20 minutes and they also had a photographer and a pianist for 30 schillings extra who played a piece from *The Magic Flute*. David says, 'We had to get two witnesses so the translator, who was there because the service was in German, was one witness and a lady who worked at the registry office was the other.'

Afterwards David and Kerrie took a horse and carriage ride and had lunch at one of Vienna's most famous restaurants then spent the night in a five-star hotel. David says, 'It was very personal but it was a beautiful day. I don't think I regret a minute of it. I wouldn't do it any other way.'

Eloping locally

When Patty and Mike decided to marry, they chose to elope. They didn't go very far though. They just drove to a historic homestead about an hour from the centre of Melbourne. Patty came from a large family and Mike's family was very complicated. Mike says, 'It would have been too hard to please everybody so we just decided to please ourselves'.

They married at a five-star resort with a beautiful restaurant in country Victoria and invited their two dearest friends to act as witnesses. They had a quiet ceremony, beautiful photos taken and had a gorgeous meal. After the ceremony they went off on their honeymoon and sent invitations to their friends inviting them to a party. At that party they did a renewal of vows. Patty says, 'It was my perfect day and my perfect dream, I wouldn't change a thing.'

Mind you, the groom's mother is still recovering as it was her only chance at a wedding—Mike was her only son! As Mum says, 'Yes, you must do what you want, but somewhere in your heart you must find a bit of room to think about what your parents want.'

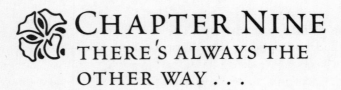 Chapter Nine
THERE'S ALWAYS THE OTHER WAY . . .

A major reason why some of us never marry is that it is too darn expensive. With the average cost of a wedding spiralling into the thousands, it seems crazy to blow so much money on one day. For some, therefore, the idea of marrying on the cheap is most attractive. There are some celebrants out there who charge a flat fee for service. However, the cheapest way to get married is to go to the registry office. Registry weddings are also to the point and easy to organise.

Going to the registry office

If you want a civil service plus a small and contained wedding and ceremony, then get married at the registry office. A registry office is an arm of the government that, basically, provides couples with the opportunity to marry in capital cities and some regional centres, simply and without burning a huge hole in their collective pocket.

In Sydney, for example, you can marry in the middle of the city with up to twelve guests. The registry provides the marriage vows and the ceremony takes approximately 15–20 minutes. The fee (for lodging your Notice of Intended Marriage form and for the ceremony) is A$335.50. In South Australia, a similar service will cost you A$165; while in New Zealand, a registry office marriage will set you back NZ$170. It's clearly a very attractive option if you are concerned about saving money and if you want a low key, speedy service.

Why the registry office?

After returning from an expensive but fun jaunt overseas, Pery and Gloria decided to get married. The next issue was where? Gloria says they had two options: the full-on Catholic white wedding or the registry office. 'We didn't have any money left so it was either start saving for two years for the church wedding or just do a small wedding now. And with our friends and family, if you have a church wedding you have to invite everybody—you can't leave anyone out—so it would have cost us tens of thousands.'

So Gloria and Pery chose to save their money for a house deposit and marry at a registry office. 'It sounds awful but it was practical,' Gloria says. They were limited to 30 people and so chose a weekday because they knew that fewer people would be able to make it. It also meant that the registry office was quieter.

What was it like?

Pery and Gloria didn't have much input into the service. It was a standard service. Pery says, 'They were kind of hard-nosed. It was like the wedding-process centre. It didn't matter though. We were really happy. It worked out really well.'

What was the fall-out?

Gloria says her mum 'freaked' when she told her she was marrying at a registry office and a lot of people 'were a little put out' because they weren't invited. 'It was a major trauma but maybe that made me dig my heels in and say, "Nuh—I don't want a church now, I want a registry wedding." '

Pery says that, while they saved a lot of money, 'the most important thing is that we are married'. 'I would have loved a big church wedding,' he says. 'I still think it is important. We'd like to get married one day in a church, to be officiated by a priest—maybe in our next lifetime.'

Maybe the registry office is the right place for you. If it is, please see Chapter 11 for contact details.

CHAPTER TEN
SOURCES OF INSPIRATION

Most couples have no idea what their favourite song is, or their favourite poem. Or if they do, it may not be the most appropriate tune or verse for a wedding ceremony. For example, how would granny react to the words of AC/DCs 'Big Balls' coming through the loud speaker? Listed below are all sorts of ideas for movies, song titles, verse and poems that you may find resonate with you or set you on the path to finding the perfect song and so on.

Movies

Casablanca
The Wedding Singer
An Affair to Remember
Love Actually
Amélie
A Room with a View
The Double Life of Veronique
Diva
Cyrano de Bergerac

Bridget Jones's Diary
Dirty Dancing—daggy but a goodie
Strictly Ballroom
Romeo and Juliet
Moulin Rouge
When Harry Met Sally
Three Colours/Red/White/Blue
The English Patient
Sabrina—with Audrey Hepburn
Breakfast at Tiffany's
Goodfella's—for the lads when they've had enough of chick flicks

Songs

Please note, I have listed the singers, not necessarily the composers, of the songs.

Jazz standards

'As Time Goes By' by Rod Stewart
'At Last' by Etta James—used in the movie *Father of the Bride* 2
'Come Rain Or Come Shine' by Ray Charles—Meryl Streep sang a
  cover of this in the movie *Postcards from the Edge*
'Fly Me To The Moon' by Michael Bublé or Frank Sinatra
'I Get A Kick Out of You' by Frank Sinatra
'It Had To Be You' by Frank Sinatra/Harry Connick Jr
'Let's Do It (Let's fall in love)' by Louis Armstrong
'L-O-V-E' by Nat King Cole
'More' by Bobby Darin
'My Baby Just Cares For Me' by Nina Simone
'The Nearness Of You' by Norah Jones/Sarah Vaughn
'Our Love is Here to Stay' by Carmen McRae
'Someone To Watch Over Me' by Frank Sinatra
'The Way You Look Tonight' by Harry Connick Jr
'Unforgettable' by Nat King Cole
'When I Fall In Love' by Nat King Cole

All-time greats

'All You Need Is Love' by The Beatles—used to great effect in the
  movie *Love Actually*
'Can't Help Falling In Love' by Elvis Presley
'Close To You' by The Carpenters
'Love Me Tender' by Elvis Presley
'Unchained Melody' by The Righteous Brothers
'I Feel Good' by James Brown
'I Only Have Eyes For You' by The Flamingos
'I Only Want To Be With You' by Bay City Rollers
'In My Life' by The Beatles
'Moondance' by Van Morrison

'Something' by The Beatles
'The Long And Winding Road' by The Beatles
'The Look Of Love' by Dusty Springfield
'We've Got Tonight' by Bob Seger
'We've Only Just Begun' by The Carpenters
'You Are So Beautiful' by Joe Cocker

Soul food

'Ain't Nobody' by Chaka Khan
'Crazy In Love' by Beyonce
'Here And Now' by Luther Vandross
'I Need Love' by LL Cool J
'Just The Two of Us' by Grover Washington Jr
'Let's Get It On' by Marvin Gaye
'Let's Stay Together' by Al Green
'My Cherie Amour' by Stevie Wonder
'Sweet Love' by Anita Baker
'The First Time Ever I Saw Your Face' by Roberta Flack
'Thinking Of You' by Sister Sledge
'Tonight I Celebrate My Love For You' by Roberta Flack and Peabo
    Bryson
'Wonderful World' by Sam Cook
'You're The First, My Last, My Everything' by Barry White
'When A Man Loves A Woman' by Percy Sledge
'You Are The Sunshine Of My Life' by Stevie Wonder
'You Sexy Thing' by Hot Chocolate

Love sick

'All My Life' by K-Ci and JoJo
'Endless Love' by Diana Ross and Lionel Ritchie
'Fields of Gold' by Sting
'From This Moment On' by Shania Twain
'Have I Told You Lately That I Love You?' by Van Morrison
'I Will Always Love You' by Whitney Houston
'Lady In Red' by Chris DeBurgh
'My Heart Will Go On' by Celine Dion
'Open Arms' by Journey

'Save The Best For Last' by Vanessa Williams
'Someone Like You' by John Waite
'The Most Beautiful Girl In The World' by Prince
'The Sweetest Thing' by U2
'The Power Of Two' by Indigo Girls
'This Guy Is In Love With You' by Herb Alpert
'True' by Spandau Ballet
'True Colours' by Cyndi Lauper or Kasey Chambers
'Up Where We Belong' by Joe Cocker and Jennifer Warrens
'Your Love Is King' by Sade
'You Are Beautiful In My Eyes' by Joshua Kadison
'You're In My Heart' by Rod Stewart
'You're Still The One' by Shania Twain
'Your Song' by Elton John

Rock on

'Are You Gonna Be My Girl?' by Jet
'(Baby I've Got You) On My Mind' by Powderfinger
'Foxy Lady' by Jimi Hendrix
'I Don't Want To Miss A Thing' by Aerosmith
'I'll Stand By You' by The Pretenders
'Into My Arms' by Nick Cave
'Love Will Never Tear Us Apart' by INXS
'Lovesong' by The Cure
'Nothing Else Matters' by Metallica
'Real Love' by Tex Perkins
'Sweet Child of Mine' by Guns and Roses
'The Ship Song' by Nick Cave
'Throw Your Arms Around Me' by Hunters and Collectors
'Wonderwall' by Oasis
'You Are My Everything' by REM
'You Shook Me All Night Long' by AC DC

Groovetrain

'I Want You' by Elvis Costello
'Protection' by Massive Attack
'Safe From Harm' by Massive Attack

'Sonnet' by The Verve
'Unfinished Sympathies' by Massive Attack

Bossa

'No More Blues' by Dizzy Gillespie
'The Girl From Ipanema' by Antonio Carlos Jobim
'Summer Samba (So Nice)' by Astrud Gilberto
'O Morro Nao Tem Vez (Favela)' by Stan Getz and Luiz Bonfa
'Wave' by Oscar Peterson

Classical

'Aria' from *La Wally*—from the *Diva* movie soundtrack
'Arrival of the Queen of Sheba' by Handel
'Ave Maria' by Schubert—used in the movie *Muriel's Wedding*
Lakme by Delibes
Canon in D by Pachelbel
The Four Seasons by Vivaldi
Trumpet Voluntary in D Major—Purcell

Defies categorisation

'Bob the Builder—Can we fix it? Why, yes we can!'—has been used
in a wedding

Songbooks

Air
Antonio Carlos Jobim
Bob Marley
Burt Bacharach
Coldplay
Ben Harper
Diana Krall
Dido
Elton John/Bernie Taupin
Elvis
Elvis Costello

Eva Cassidy
Frank Sinatra
Jimi Hendrix
Joni Mitchell
Johnny Mercer
Michael Bublé
Motley Crue—for the metal heads
Nat King Cole
Neil Finn
Norah Jones
Rickie Lee Jones
Rogers and Hart
Sarah Vaughn
Serge Gainsbourg
The Beatles
U2
Van Morrison

Movie soundtracks

A Room With a View
The Big Chill—60s classics
Buena Vista Social Club
Any Quentin Tarantino, Baz Luhrmann or Cameron Crowe movie
Something's Gotta Give
When Harry Met Sally

Readings and poems

Golden oldies

'Sonnet 17' by William Shakespeare

If I could write the beauty of your eyes
And in fresh numbers number all your graces,
The age to come would say 'This poet lies:
Such heavenly touches ne'er touched earthly faces.'

Twelfth Night by William Shakespeare

A contract of eternal bond of love,
Confirmed by mutual joinder of your hands,
Attested by the holy close of lips.
Strengthened by interchangement of your rings,
And all the ceremony of this compact
sealed in my function,
By my testimony.

'Shall I Compare Thee' ('Sonnet 18') by William Shakespeare

Shall I compare thee to a summer's day?
Thou art more lovely and more temperate:
Rough winds do shake the darling buds of May,
And summer's lease hath all too short a date:
Sometime too hot the eye of heaven shines,
And often is his gold complexion dimm'd;
And every fair from fair sometime declines,
By chance or nature's changing course untrimm'd:
But thy eternal Summer shall not fade,
Nor lose possession of that fair thou owest;
Nor shall Death brag thou wander'st in his shade,
When in eternal lines to time thou grow'st:
So long as men can breathe, or eyes can see,
So long lives this, and this gives life to thee.

'Let Me Not to the Marriage of True Minds' ('Sonnet 116') by William Shakespeare

Let me not to the marriage of true minds
Admit impediments. Love is not love
Which alters when it alteration finds,
Or bends with the remover to remove:
O, no! it is an ever-fixed mark,
That looks on tempests and is never shaken;
It is the star to every wandering bark,
Whose worth's unknown, although his height be taken.
Love's not Time's fool, though rosy lips and cheeks
Within his bending sickle's compass come;
Love alters not with his brief hours and weeks,
But bears it out even to the edge of doom.
If this be error and upon me proved,
I never writ, nor no man ever loved.

Hamlet by William Shakespeare

Doubt thou the stars are fire;
Doubt that the sun doth move;
Doubt truth to be a liar;
But never doubt I love.

Sonnets from the Portuguese, 43: by Elizabeth Barrett Browning

How do I love thee? Let me count the ways.
I love thee to the depth and breadth and height
My soul can reach, when feeling out of sight
For the ends of being and ideal grace.
I love thee to the level of everyday's
Most quiet need, by sun and candlelight.
I love thee freely, as men strive for right;
I love thee purely, as they turn from praise.
I love thee with the passion put to use
In my old griefs, and with my childhood's faith.
I love thee with a love I seemed to lose

With my lost saints,—love thee with the breath,
Smiles, tears, of all my life; and, if God choose,
I shall but love thee better after death.

Sonnets from the Portuguese, 14 by Elizabeth Barret Browning

If thou must love me, let it be for nought
Except for love's sake only. Do not say
'I love her for her smile—her look—her way
Of speaking gently,—for a trick of thought
That falls in well with mine, and certes brought
A sense of pleasant ease on such a day'—
For these things in themselves, Beloved, may
Be changed, or change for thee,—and love,
    so wrought,
May be unwrought so. Neither love me for
Thine own dear pity's wiping my cheeks dry,—
A creature might forget to weep, who bore
Thy comfort long, and lose thy love thereby!
But love me for love's sake, that evermore
Thou may'st love on, through love's eternity.

'He Wishes for the Cloths of Heaven' by WB Yeats

Had I the heavens' embroidered cloths,
Enwrought with golden and silver light,
The blue and the dim and the dark cloths
Of night and light and the half-light,
I would spread the cloths under your feet:
But I, being poor, have only my dreams;
I have spread my dreams under your feet;
Tread softly because you tread on my dreams.

'Song: to Celia' by Ben Jonson

Drink to me only with thine eyes,
And I will pledge with mine;
Or leave a kiss but in the cup,
And I'll not look for wine.

The thirst that from the soul doth rise,
Doth ask a drink divine;
But might I of Jove's nectar sup,
I would not change for thine.

I sent thee late a rosy wreath,
Not so much honoring thee,
As giving it a hope that there
It could not withered be.
But thou thereon didst only breathe,
And send'st it back to me:
Since when it grows, and smells, I swear,
Not of itself, but thee.

'My Love is Like a Red, Red Rose' by Robert Burns

O, My luve is like a red, red rose,
That's newly sprung in June;
O my Luve is like the melodie
That's sweetly play'd in tune.
As fair art thou, my bonnie lass,
So deep in luve am I;
And I will luve thee still, my dear,
Till a'the seas gang dry.
Till a'the seas gang dry, my dear,
And the rocks melt wi'the sun:
And I luve thee still, my dear,
While the sands o'life shall run.
And fare thee weel, my only Luve,
And fare thee weel awhile!
And I will come again, my Luve,
Though it were ten thousand mile.

'To His Coy Mistress' by Andrew Marvell

Had we but world enough and time
This coyness, Lady, were no crime.
We would sit down, and think which way
To walk, and pass our long love's day,

Thou by the Indian Ganges' side
Shouldst rubies find: I by the tide
Of Humber would complain. I would
Love you ten years before the flood:
And you should, if you please, refuse
Till the conversion of the Jews.
My vegetable love should grow
Vaster than empires and more slow;
An hundred years should go to praise
Thine eyes and on thy forehead gaze;
Two hundred to adore each breast:
But thirty thousand to the rest;
An age at least to every part,
And the last age should show your heart:
For, Lady, you deserve this state;
Nor would I love at lower rate.

But at my back I always hear
Time's wingéd chariot hurrying near:
And yonder all before us lie
Deserts of vast eternity.
Thy beauty shall no more be found,
Nor, in thy marble vault, shall sound
My echoing song; then worms shall try
That long preserved virginity:
And your quaint honor turn to dust;
And into ashes all my lust.
The grave's a fine and private place,
But none, I think, do there embrace.

Now therefore, while the youthful hue
Sits on thy skin like morning dew,
And while thy willing soul transpires
At every pore with instant fires,
Now let us sport us while we may;
And now, like amorous birds of prey,
Rather at once our time devour,
Than languish in his slow-chapped power.
Let us roll all our strength, and all

Our sweetness up into one ball:
And tear our pleasures with rough strife,
Thorough the iron gates of life.
Thus, though we cannot make our sun
Stand still, yet we will make him run.

'The Passionate Shepherd to His Love' by Christopher Marlowe

Come live with me, and be my Love,
And we will all the pleasures prove
That hills and valleys, dale and field,
And all the craggy mountain yields.

There will we sit upon the rocks
And see the shepherds feed their flocks,
By shallow rivers, to whose falls
Melodious birds sing madrigals.

There will I make thee beds of roses,
And a thousand fragrant posies,
A cap of flowers, and a kirtle,
Embroidered all with leaves of myrtle.

A gown made of the finest wool
Which from our pretty lambs we pull,
Fair lined slippers for the cold,
With buckles of the purest gold.

A belt of straw and ivy buds,
With coral clasps and amber studs,
And if these pleasures may thee move,
Come live with me, and be my love.

The shepherds' swains shall dance and sing
For thy delight each May morning;
If these delights thy mind may move,
Then live with me, and be my love.

'That Love is All There Is' by Emily Dickinson

That Love is all there is,
Is all we know of Love;
It is enough, the freight should be
Proportioned to the groove.

'She Walks in Beauty!' by Lord Byron

She walks in beauty, like the night
Of cloudless climes and starry skies;
And all that's best of dark and bright
Meet on her aspect and her eyes:
Thus mellow'd to that tender light
Which heaven to gaudy day denies.

One shade the more, one ray the less,
Had half impair'd the nameless grace
Which waves in every raven tress,
Or softly lightens o'er her face;
Where thoughts serenely sweet express
How pure, how dear their dwelling-place.

And on that cheek, and o'er that brow,
So soft, so calm, yet eloquent,
The smiles that win, the tints that glow,
But tell of days in goodness spent,
A mind at peace with all below,
A heart whose love is innocent!

'When You are Old' by WB Yeats

When you are old and gray and full of sleep
And nodding by the fire, take down this book,
And slowly read, and dream of the soft look
Your eyes had once, and of their shadows deep;

How many loved your moments of glad grace,
And loved your beauty with love false or true;

But one man loved the pilgrim soul in you,
And loved the sorrows of your changing face.

And bending down beside the glowing bars,
Murmur, a little sadly, how Love fled
And paced upon the mountains overhead,
And hid his face amid a crowd of stars.

'Will You Give Me Yourself' by Walt Whitman

I give you my love, more precious than money,
I give you myself before preaching or law;
Will you give me yourself?
Will you come travel with me?
Shall we stick by each other as long as we live?

'Fidelity' by DH Lawrence

Man and woman are like the earth, that brings forth flowers
in summer, and love, but underneath is rock.
Older than flowers, older than ferns, older than foraminiferae,
older than plasm altogether is the soul underneath.
And when, throughout all the wild chaos of love
slowly a gem forms, in the ancient, once-more-molten rocks
of two human hearts, two ancient rocks,
a man's heart and a woman's,
that is the crystal of peace, the slow hard jewel of trust,
the sapphire of fidelity.
The gem of mutual peace emerging from the wild chaos of love.

'The First Day' by Christina Rossetti

I wish I could remember the first day
First hour, first moment of your meeting me,
If bright or dim the season, it might be
Summer or winter for aught I can say.
So unrecorded did it slip away,
So blind was I to see and to foresee,
So dull to mark the budding of my tree
That would not blossom for many a May.

If only I could recollect it! Such
A day of days! I let it come and go
As traceless as a thaw of bygone snow.
It seemed to mean so little, meant so much!
If only now I could recall that touch,
First touch of hand in hand!—Did one but know.

'Night Thoughts' by Johann Wolfgang von Goethe

Stars, you are unfortunate, I pity you,
Beautiful as you are, shining in your glory,
Who guide seafaring men through stress and peril
And have no recompense from gods or mortals,
Love you do not, nor do you know what love is.
Hours that are aeons urgently conducting
Your figures in a dance through the vast heaven,
What journey have you ended in this moment,
Since lingering in the arms of my beloved
I lost all memory of you and midnight.

'Into the Mystic' from the *I Ching*

When two people are at one
in their inmost hearts,
They shatter even the strength of iron or bronze.
And when two people understand each other
in their inmost hearts,
Their words are sweet and strong,
like the fragrance of orchids.

Hindu marriage poem

You have become mine forever.
Yes, we have become partners.
I have become yours.
Hereafter, I cannot live without you.
Do not live without me.
Let us share the joys.
We are word and meaning, united.
You are thought and I am sound.

May the nights be honey-sweet for us.
May the mornings be honey-sweet for us.
May the plants be honey-sweet for us.
May the earth be honey-sweet for us.

'On Marriage' by Kahlil Gibran

Then Almitra spoke again and said, 'And
what of Marriage, master?'
And he answered saying:
You were born together, and together you
shall be forevermore.
You shall be together when white wings
of death scatter your days.
Aye, you shall be together even in the
silent memory of God.
But let there be spaces in your togetherness,
And let the winds of the heavens dance between you.
Love one another but make not a bond of love:
Let it rather be a moving sea between the shores of your souls.
Fill each other's cup but drink not from one cup.
Give one another of your bread but eat not from the same loaf.
Sing and dance together and be joyous, but let each one of you be
    alone,
Even as the strings of a lute are alone though they quiver with the
    same music.
Give your hearts, but not into each other's keeping.
For only the hand of Life can contain your hearts.
And stand together, yet not too near together:
For the pillars of the temple stand apart,
And the oak tree and the cypress grow not in each other's shadow.

'Married Love' by Kuan Tao-Sheng

You and I
Have so much love
That it
Burns like fire,
In which we bake a lump of clay

Moulded into a figure of you
And a figure of me.
Then we take both of them,
And break them into pieces,
and mix the pieces with water,
and mould again a figure of you
And a figure of me.
I am in your clay,
You are in my clay

Modern Classics

'Warming Her Pearls' by Carol Ann Duffy

Next to my own skin, her pearls. My mistress
bids me wear them, warm then, until evening
when I'll brush her hair. At six, I place them
round her cool, white throat. All day I think of her,

resting in the Yellow Room, contemplating silk
or taffeta, which gown tonight? She fans herself
whilst I work willingly, my slow heat entering
each pearl. Slack on my neck, her rope.

She's beautiful. I dream about her
in my attic bed; picture her dancing
with tall men, puzzled by my faint, persistent scent
beneath her French perfume, her milky stones.

I dust her shoulders with a rabbit's foot,
watch the soft blush seep through her skin
like an indolent sigh. In her looking-glass
my red lips part as though I want to speak.

Full moon. Her carriage brings her home. I see
her every movement in my head . . . Undressing,
taking off her jewels, her slim hand reaching
for the case, slipping naked into bed, the way

she always does . . . And I lie here awake,
knowing the pearls are cooling even now
in the room where my mistress sleeps. All night
I feel their absence and I burn.

'I Wanna Be Yours' by John Cooper Clarke

I wanna be your vacuum cleaner
Breathing in your dust,
I wanna be your Ford Cortina
I will never rust,
If you like your coffee hot
let me be your coffee pot,
You call the shots,
I wanna be yours.

I wanna be your raincoat
For those frequent rainy days,
I wanna be your dreamboat
When you want to sail away,
Let me be your teddy bear
Take me with you anywhere,
I don't care,
I wanna be yours.

I wanna be your electric meter
I will not run out,
I wanna be the electric heater
You'll get cold without,
I wanna be your setting lotion
Hold your hair in deep devotion,
Deep as the deep Atlantic ocean
That's how deep is my devotion.

'The Invitation' by Oriah Mountain Dreamer

It doesn't interest me what you do for a living.
I want to know what you ache for, and if you dare to dream of
meeting your heart's longing.

It doesn't interest me how old you are.
I want to know if you will risk looking like a fool for love, for your dream, for the adventure of being alive.

It doesn't interest me what planets are squaring your moon . . .
I want to know if you have touched the centre of your own sorrow if you have been opened by life's betrayals or have become shrivelled and closed from fear of further pain!
I want to know if you can sit with pain, mine or your own, without moving to hide it or fade it, or fix it.

I want to know if you can be with joy, mine or your own, if you can dance with wildness and let ecstasy fill you to the tips of your fingers and toes without cautioning us to be careful, be realistic, or to remember the limitations of being human.

It doesn't interest me if the story you are telling me is true.
I want to know if you can disappoint another to be true to yourself.
If you can bear the accusation of betrayal and not betray your own soul. If you can be faithful and therefore trustworthy.
I want to know if you can see beauty even if its not pretty every day, and if you can source your own life from its presence.
I want to know if you can live with failure, yours and mine, and still stand on the edge of a lake and shout to the silver moon, 'Yes!'

It doesn't interest me to know where you live or how much money you have.
I want to know if you can get up after the night of grief and despair, weary, bruised to the bone, and do what needs to be done to feed the children.

It doesn't interest me who you know, or how you came to be here. I want to know if you will stand in the centre of the fire with me and not shrink back.

It doesn't interest me where or what or with whom you have studied.
I want to know what sustains you from the inside, when all else falls away.

I want to know if you can be alone with yourself and if you truly like the company you keep in the empty moments.

'Love Should Grow Up Like a Wild Iris in the Fields' by Susan Griffin

Love should grow up like a wild iris in the fields,
unexpected, after a terrible storm, opening a purple
mouth to the rain, with not a thought to the future,
ignorant of the grass and the graveyard of leaves
around, forgetting its own beginning. Love should
grow like a wild iris
but it does not.
Love more often is to be found in kitchens at the dinner hour,
tired out and hungry, lingers over tables in houses where
the walls record movements; while the cook is probably angry,
and the ingredients of the meal are budgeted, while
a child cries feed me now and her mother not quite
hysterical says over and over, wait just a bit, just a bit.
Love should grow up in the fields like a wild iris
but never does
really startle anyone, was to be expected, was to be
predicted, is almost absurd, goes on from day to day, not quite
blindly, gets taken to the cleaners every fall, sings
old songs over and over, and falls in the same piece of rug that
never gets tacked down, gives up, wants to hide, is not
brave, knows too much, is not like an
iris growing wild but more like
staring into space
in the street
not quite sure
which door it was, annoyed about the sidewalk being
slippery, trying all the doors, thinking
if love wished the world to be well, it would be well.
Love should
grow up like a wild iris, but doesn't, it comes from
the midst of everything else, see like the iris
of an eye, when the light is right,
fells in blindness and when there is nothing else is

tender, blinks and opens
face up to the skies.

'The Voyage' by Johnny Duhan

I am a sailor, you're my first mate
We signed on together, we coupled our fate
Hauled up our anchor, determined not to fail
For the hearts treasure, together we set sail
With no maps to guide us we steered our own course
Rode out the storms when the winds were gale force
Sat out the doldrums in patience and hope
Working together we learned how to cope
Chorus:
Life is an ocean and love is a boat
In troubled water that keeps us afloat
When we started the voyage, there was just me and you
Now gathered round us, we have our own crew
Together we're in this relationship
We built it with care to last the whole trip
Our true destination's not marked on any charts
We're navigating to the shores of the heart.

'Grow Old Along with Me' by John Lennon

Grow old along with me
The best is yet to be
When our time has come
We will be as one
God bless our love
God bless our love
Grow old go on with me
Two branches are one tree
Face the setting sun
When the day is done
God bless our love
God bless our love
Spending our lives together
Man and the wife together

World without hurt
World without hate
Grow old along with me
Whatever fate decrees
We'll see it thru
For our love is true
God bless our love
God bless our love

'The Silken Tent' by Robert Frost

She is as in a field a silken tent
At midday when the sunny summer breeze
Has dried the dew and all its ropes relent,
So that in guys it gently sways at ease,
And its supporting central cedar pole,
That is its pinnacle to heavenward
And signifies the sureness of the soul,
Seems to owe naught to any single cord,
But strictly held by none, is loosely bound
By countless silken ties of love and thought
To everything on earth the compass round,
And only by one's going slightly taut
In the capriciousness of summer air
Is of the slightest bondage made aware.

'Lullaby' by WH Auden

Lay your sleeping head, my love,
Human on my faithless arm;
Time and fevers burn away
Individual beauty from
Thoughtful children, and the grave
Proves the child ephemeral:
But in my arms till break of day
Let the living creature lie,
Mortal, guilty, but to me
The entirely beautiful.

Soul and body have no bounds:
To lovers as they lie upon
Her tolerant enchanted slope
In their ordinary swoon,
Grave the vision Venus sends
Of supernatural sympathy,
Universal love and hope;
While an abstract insight wakes
Among the glaciers and the rocks
The hermit's carnal ecstasy.

Certainty, fidelity
On the stroke of midnight pass
Like vibrations of a bell
And fashionable madmen raise
Their pedantic boring cry:
Every farthing cost,
All the dreaded cards foretell,
Shall be paid, but from this night
Not a whisper, not a thought,
Not a kiss nor look be lost.

Beauty, midnight, vision dies:
Let the winds of dawn that blow
Softly round your dreaming head
Such a day of welcome show
Eye and knocking heart may bless,
Find our mortal world enough;
Noons of dryness find you fed
By the involuntary powers,
Nights of insult let you pass
Watched by every human love.

'i carry your heart with me' by e.e. cummings

i carry your heart with me (i carry it in
my heart) i am never without it (anywhere
i go you go, my dear; and whatever is done
by only me is your doing, my darling)

i fear
no fate (for you are my fate, my sweet) i want
no world (for beautiful you are my world, my true)
and it's you are whatever a moon has always meant
and whatever a sun will always sing is you

here is the deepest secret nobody knows
(here is the root of the root and the bud of the bud
and the sky of the sky of a tree called life; which grows
higher than soul can hope or mind can hide)
and this is the wonder that's keeping the stars apart

i carry your heart (i carry it in my heart)

'O Tell Me the Truth about Love' by WH Auden

Some say love's a little boy,
And some say it's a bird,
Some say it makes the world go around,
Some say that's absurd,
And when I asked the man next-door,
Who looked as if he knew,
His wife got very cross indeed,
And said it wouldn't do.

Does it look like a pair of pyjamas,
Or the ham in a temperance hotel?
Does its odour remind one of llamas,
Or has it a comforting smell?
Is it prickly to touch as a hedge is,
Or soft as eiderdown fluff?
Is it sharp or quite smooth at the edges?
O tell me the truth about love.

Our history books refer to it
In cryptic little notes,
It's quite a common topic on
The Transatlantic boats;
I've found the subject mentioned in

Accounts of suicides,
And even seen it scribbled on
The backs of railway guides.

Does it howl like a hungry Alsatian,
Or boom like a military band?
Could one give a first-rate imitation
On a saw or a Steinway Grand?
Is its singing at parties a riot?
Does it only like Classical stuff?
Will it stop when one wants to be quiet?
O tell me the truth about love.

I looked inside the summer-house;
It wasn't over there;
I tried the Thames at Maidenhead,
And Brighton's bracing air.
I don't know what the blackbird sang,
Or what the tulip said;
But it wasn't in the chicken-run,
Or underneath the bed.

Can it pull extraordinary faces?
Is it usually sick on a swing?
Does it spend all its time at the races,
or fiddling with pieces of string?
Has it views of its own about money?
Does it think Patriotism enough?
Are its stories vulgar but funny?
O tell me the truth about love.

When it comes, will it come without warning
Just as I'm picking my nose?
Will it knock on my door in the morning,
Or tread in the bus on my toes?
Will it come like a change in the weather?
Will its greeting be courteous or rough?
Will it alter my life altogether?
O tell me the truth about love.

'As I Walked Out One Evening' by WH Auden

As I walked out one evening,
Walking down Bristol Street,
The crowds upon the pavement
Were fields of harvest wheat.

And down by the brimming river
I heard a lover sing
Under an arch of the railway:
'Love has no ending.

'I'll love you, dear, I'll love you
Till China and Africa meet,
And the river jumps over the mountain
And the salmon sing in the street,

'I'll love you till the ocean
Is folded and hung up to dry
And the seven stars go squawking
Like geese about the sky.

'The years shall run like rabbits,
For in my arms I hold
The Flower of the Ages,
And the first love of the world.'

But all the clocks in the city
Began to whirr and chime:
'O let not Time deceive you,
You cannot conquer Time.

'In the burrows of the Nightmare
Where Justice naked is,
Time watches from the shadow
And coughs when you would kiss.

'In headaches and in worry
Vaguely life leaks away,

And Time will have his fancy
To-morrow or to-day.

'Into many a green valley
Drifts the appalling snow;
Time breaks the threaded dances
And the diver's brilliant bow.

'O plunge your hands in water,
Plunge them in up to the wrist;
Stare, stare in the basin
And wonder what you've missed.

'The glacier knocks in the cupboard,
The desert sighs in the bed,
And the crack in the tea-cup opens
A lane to the land of the dead.

'Where the beggars raffle the banknotes
And the Giant is enchanting to Jack,
And the Lily-white Boy is a Roarer,
And Jill goes down on her back.

'O look, look in the mirror?
O look in your distress:
Life remains a blessing
Although you cannot bless.

'O stand, stand at the window
As the tears scald and start;
You shall love your crooked neighbour
With your crooked heart.'

It was late, late in the evening,
The lovers they were gone;
The clocks had ceased their chiming,
And the deep river ran on.

'Us Two' by AA Milne

Wherever I am, there's always Pooh,
There's always Pooh and Me.
Whatever I do, he wants to do,
'Where are you going today?' says Pooh:
'Well, that's very odd 'cos I was too.
'Let's go together,' says Pooh, says he.
'Let's go together,' says Pooh.

'What's twice eleven?' I said to Pooh.
('Twice what?' said Pooh to Me.)
'I think it ought to be twenty-two.'
'Just what I think myself,' said Pooh.
'It wasn't an easy sum to do,
But that's what it is,' said Pooh, said he.
'That's what it is,' said Pooh.

'Let's look for dragons,' I said to Pooh.
'Yes, let's,' said Pooh to Me.
We crossed the river and found a few—
'Yes, those are dragons all right,' said Pooh.
'As soon as I saw their beaks I knew.
That's what they are,' said Pooh, said he.
'That's what they are,' said Pooh.

'Let's frighten the dragons,' I said to Pooh.
'That's right,' said Pooh to Me.
'I'm not afraid,' I said to Pooh,
And I held his paw and I shouted 'Shoo!
Silly old dragons!'—and off they flew.

'I wasn't afraid,' said Pooh, said he,
'I'm never afraid with you.'

So wherever I am, there's always Pooh,
There's always Pooh and Me.
'What would I do?' I said to Pooh,
'If it wasn't for you,' and Pooh said: 'True,

It isn't much fun for One, but Two,
Can stick together' says Pooh, says he. 'That's how it is,' says Pooh.

'The Curve of Your Eyes . . . ' by Paul Eluard

The curve of your eyes moves in orbit round my heart
A round of dance and gentleness,
Halo of time, safe nocturnal cradle,
And if I know no longer all that I have lived
It is because your eyes have not always seen me.
Leaves of day and froth of dew,
Reeds of the wind, scented smiles,
Wings spreading a mantle of light over the world
Boats laden with the sky and the sea,
Hunters of sound and springs of colours,
Perfumes hatched out from a brood of dawns
That lies for ever on the straw of stars,
As daylight depends on innocence
The whole world depends on your pure eyes
And all my blood flows into their gaze.

'Bride and Groom Lie Hidden for Three Days' by Ted Hughes

She gives him his eyes, she found them
Among some rubble, among some beetles

He gives her her skin
He just seemed to pull it down out of the air and lay it over her
She weeps with fearfulness and astonishment

She has found his hands for him, and fitted them freshly at the wrists
They are amazed at themselves, they go feeling all over her

He has assembled her spine, he cleaned each piece carefully
And sets them in perfect order
A superhuman puzzle but he is inspired
She leans back twisting this way and that, using it and laughing
Incredulous

Now she has brought his feet, she is connecting them
So that his whole body lights up

And he has fashioned her new hips
With all fittings complete and with newly wound coils, all
shiningly oiled
He is polishing every part, he himself can hardly believe it

They keep taking each other to the sun, they find they can easily
To test each new thing at each new step

And now she smoothes over him the plates of his skull
So that the joints are invisible

And now he connects her throat, her breasts and the pit of her
stomach
With a single wire

She gives him his teeth, tying the roots to the centrepin of his
body

He sets the little circlets on her fingertips

She stiches his body here and there with steely purple silk

He oils the delicate cogs of her mouth

She inlays with deep cut scrolls the nape of his neck

He sinks into place the inside of her thighs

So, gasping with joy, with cries of wonderment
Like two gods of mud
Sprawling in the dirt, but with infinite care
They bring each other to perfection.

'To Keep Your Marriage Brimming' by Ogden Nash

To keep your marriage brimming,
With love in the loving cup,
Whenever you're wrong admit it;
Whenever you're right shut up.

'Reprise' by Ogden Nash

Geniuses of countless nations
Have told their love for generations
Till all their memorable phrases
Are common as goldenrod or daisies.
Their girls have glimmered like the moon,
Or shimmered like a summer moon,
Stood like a lily, fled like a fawn,
Now the sunset, now the dawn,
Here the princess in the tower
There the sweet forbidden flower.
Darling, when I look at you
Every aged phrase is new,
And there are moments when it seems
I've married one of Shakespeare's dreams.

'The Owl and the Pussy-cat' by Edward Lear

The Owl and the Pussy-cat went to sea
In a beautiful pea green boat,
They took some honey, and plenty of money,
Wrapped up in a five pound note.
The Owl looked up to the stars above,
And sang to a small guitar,
'O lovely Pussy! O Pussy my love,
What a beautiful Pussy you are,
You are,
You are!
What a beautiful Pussy you are!'

Pussy said to the Owl, 'You elegant fowl!
How charmingly sweet you sing!

O let us be married! too long we have tarried:
But what shall we do for a ring?'
They sailed away, for a year and a day,
To the land where the Bong-tree grows
And there in a wood a Piggy-wig stood
With a ring at the end of his nose,
His nose,
His nose,
With a ring at the end of his nose.

'Dear Pig, are you willing to sell for one shilling
Your ring?' Said the Piggy, 'I will.'
So they took it away, and were married next day
By the Turkey who lives on the hill.
They dined on mince, and slices of quince,
Which they ate with a runcible spoon;
And hand in hand, on the edge of the sand,
They danced by the light of the moon,
The moon,
The moon,
They danced by the light of the moon.

Traditional

Blessing Engraved on Saint Patrick's Breastplate

May you be blessed with the strength of heaven,
the light of the sun and the radiance of the moon
the splendour of fire,
the speed of lightning,
the swiftness of wind,
the depth of the sea,
the stability of earth and the firmness of rock.

Traditional Irish Blessing

May the road rise to meet you,
May the wind be always at your back.
May the sun shine warm upon your face,

The rains fall soft upon your fields.
And until we meet again,
May God hold you in the palm of his hand.
May God be with you and bless you:
May you see your children's children.
May you be poor in misfortune,
Rich in blessings.
May you know nothing but happiness
From this day forward.
May the road rise up to meet you
May the wind be always at your back
May the warm rays of sun fall upon your home
And may the hand of a friend always be near.
May green be the grass you walk on,
May blue be the skies above you,
May pure be the joys that surround you,
May true be the hearts that love you.

The Apache Wedding Prayer

Now you will feel no rain,
For each of you will be shelter for the other.
Now you will feel no cold,
For each will be warmth for the other.
Now you will feel no loneliness,
For each of you will be companion to the other.
Now you are two persons,
But there are three lives before you:
His life, her life and your life together.

May beauty surround you both
On the journey ahead and through all the years.
May happiness be your companion
To the place where the river meets the sun.
Go now to your dwelling
To enter into the days of your life together.
And may your days be good
And long upon the earth.

'Let Me Walk in Beauty' from a traditional Native American prayer

O Great Spirit
Whose voice speaks in the winds,
and whose breath gives life to all the world,
hear me!
I am small and weak. I need Your power your strength and wisdom.
Let me walk in beauty and make my eyes ever
behold the red and purple sunset.
Make my hands respect the things you have made
and my ears sharp to hear your voice.
Make me wise so
that I may understand the things
you have taught my people
Let me learn the lessons you have hidden in every leaf and rock.
I seek strength
not to be greater than my brother
but to my greatest enemy—myself.
Make me always ready to come to you
with clean hands
and straight eyes,
So when life fades away as the fading sunset,
so may my spirit come to you
without shame.

Extracts from novels and writings.

'On Marriage—Letters to a young poet' by Rainer Maria Rilke

The point of marriage is not to create a quick commonality by tear-
ing down all boundaries; on the contrary, a good marriage is one in
which each partner appoints the other to be *the guardian of his solitude*, and thus they show each other the greatest possible trust. A
merging of two people is an impossibility, and where it seems to
exist, it is a hemming-in, a mutual consent that robs one party or
both parties of their fullest freedom and development. But once the
realization is accepted that even between the closest people infinite
distances exist, a marvelous living side-by-side can grow up for
them, if they succeed in loving the expanse between them, which

gives them the possibility of always seeing each other as a whole and before an immense sky.

'On Love—letters to a young poet' by Rainer Maria Rilke

For one human being to love another: that is perhaps the most difficult of all our tasks, the ultimate, the last test and proof, the work for which all other work is but preparation. For this reason young people, who are beginners in everything, cannot yet know love: they have to learn it. With their whole being, with all their forces, gathered close about their lonely, timid, upward-beating heart, they must learn to love.

A Room With a View by EM Forster

. . . It isn't possible to love and to part. You will wish that it was. You can transmute love, ignore it, muddle it, but you can never pull it out of you. I know by experience that the poets are right: love is eternal.

Beloved by Toni Morrison

Paul D sits down in the rocking chair and examines the quilt patched in carnival colours. His hands are limp between his knees. There are too many things to feel about this woman. His head hurts. Suddenly he remembers Sixo trying to describe what he felt about the Thirty-Mile Woman 'She is a friend of my mind. She gather me, man. The pieces I am, she gather them and give them back to me in all the right order. It's good, you know, when you got a woman who is a friend of your mind.'

Captain Corelli's Mandolin by Louis de Bernières

Love is a temporary madness,
it erupts like volcanoes and then subsides.
And when it subsides you have to make a decision.
You have to work out whether your roots have so entwined together
that it is inconceivable that you should ever part.
Because this is what love is.
Love is not breathlessness,

it is not excitement,
it is not the promulgation of eternal passion.
That is just being 'in love' which any fool can do.
Love itself is what is left over when being in love has burned away,
and this is both an art and a fortunate accident.
Those that truly love, have roots that grow towards each other
    underground,
and when all the pretty blossom have fallen from their branches,
they find that they are one tree and not two.

The Little Prince and the Rose by Antoine de Saint-Exupery

The little prince went away, to look again at the roses.
'You are not at all like my rose,' he said. 'As yet you are nothing. No one
has tamed you, and you have tamed no one. You are like my fox
when I first knew him. He was only a fox like a hundred thousand
other foxes. But I have made him my friend, and now he is unique
in all the world.'
And the roses were very much embarrassed.
'You are beautiful, but you are empty,' he went on. 'One could not die
for you. To be sure, an ordinary passerby would think that my rose
looked just like you—the rose that belonged to me. But in herself
alone she is more important than all the hundreds of you other
roses: because it is she that I have watered; because it is she that I
have put under the glass globe; because it is she that I have sheltered
behind the screen; because it is for her that I have killed the caterpil-
lars (except the two or three that I saved to become butterflies);
because it is she that I have listened to, when she grumbled, or
boasted, or even sometimes when she said nothing.
Because she is *my* rose.'

Victor Hugo

The supreme happiness of life is the conviction that we are loved;
loved for ourselves—say, rather, in spite of ourselves.

Australian poems

'As Long as your Eyes are Blue' by Andrew Barton 'Banjo' Paterson

Will you love me, sweet, when my hair is grey
And my cheeks shall have lost their hue?
When the charms of youth shall have passed away,
Will your love as of old prove true?

For the looks may change, and the heart may range,
And the love be no longer fond.
Will you love with truth in the years of youth
And away to the years beyond?

Oh, I love you, sweet, for your locks of brown
And the blush on your cheek that lies—
But I love you most for the kindly heart
That I see in your sweet blue eyes.
For the eyes are signs of the soul within,
Of the heart that is leal and true,
And mine own sweetheart, I shall love you still,
Just as long as your eyes are blue.
For the locks may bleach, and the cheeks of peach
May be reft of their golden hue;
But mine own sweetheart, I shall love you still,
Just as long as your eyes are blue.

'Love's Coming' by John Shaw Neilson

Quietly as rosebuds,
Talk to the thin air,
Love came so lightly
I knew not he was there.

Quietly as lovers
Creep at the middle moon,
Softly as players tremble

In the tears of a tune;
Quietly as lilies
Their faint vows declare
Came the shy pilgrim:

I knew not he was there.
Quietly as tears fall
On a warm sin,
Softly as griefs call

In a violin;
Without hail or tempest
Blue sword of flame
Love came so lightly
I knew not that he came.

New Zealand poems

'Aotearoa litany' by Anne Powell

Green of fern refresh us
Feathers of Kereru warm us
Rocks of Moeraki encircle us
Waters of Taupo bath us
Dive of gannet focus us
Arc of rainbow protect us
Stars of Southern Cross guide us.

'Camomile Tea' by Katherine Mansfield

Outside the sky is light with stars;
There's a hollow roaring from the sea.
And, alas! for the little almond flowers,
The wind is shaking the almond tree.

How little I thought, a year ago,
In the horrible cottage upon the Lee
That he and I should be sitting so
And sipping a cup of camomile tea.

Light as feathers the witches fly,
The horn of the moon is plain to see;
By a firefly under a jonquil flower
A goblin toasts a bumble-bee.

We might be fifty, we might be five,
So snug, so compact, so wise are we!
Under the kitchen-table leg
My knee is pressing against his knee.

Our shutters are shut, the fire is low,
The tap is dripping peacefully;
The saucepan shadows on the wall
Are black and round and plain to see.

See also 'Spectacular Blossom' by Allen Curnow and 'The Return' by Alistair Campbell. Also, *My Heart Goes Swimming—New Zealand Love Poems* by Jenny Bornholdt & Gregory O'Brian and *New Zealand Love Poems—An Oxford Anthology* edited by Lauris Edmond.

Religious

A reading from the first letter of St Paul to the Corinthians 12:31 – 13:8 (ESV)

Be ambitious for the higher gifts. And I am going to show you the way that is better than any of them. If I have all the eloquence of men or of angels, but speak without love, I am simply a gong booming or a cymbal clashing. If I have the gift of prophecy, understanding all the mysteries there are, and knowing everything, and if I have faith in all its fullness, to move mountains, but without love, then I am nothing at all. If I give away all that I possess, piece by piece, and if I even let them take my body to burn it, but am without love, it will do me no good whatever. Love is always patient and kind; it is never jealous; love is never boastful or conceited; it is never rude or selfish; it does not take offence, and is not resentful. Love takes no pleasure in others' sins but delights in the truth; it is always ready to excuse, to trust, to hope, and to endure whatever comes.

'On Love' by Thomas à Kempis

Love is a mighty power, a great and complete good.
Love alone lightens every burden, and makes rough places smooth.
It bears every hardship as though it were nothing, and renders all
    bitterness sweet and acceptable.
Nothing is sweeter than love,
Nothing stronger,
Nothing higher,
Nothing wider,
Nothing more pleasant,
Nothing fuller or better in heaven or earth;
for love is born of God
Love flies, runs and leaps for joy.
It is free and unrestrained.
Love knows no limits, but ardently transcends all bounds.
Love feels no burden, takes no account of toil,
attempts things beyond its strength.
Love sees nothing as impossible,
for it feels able to achieve all things.
It is strange and effective,
while those who lack love faint and fail.
Love is not fickle and sentimental,
nor is it intent on vanities.
Like a living flame and a burning torch,
it surges upward and surely surmounts every obstacle.

'The Prayer' by St Francis of Assisi

Lord, make us instruments of your peace.
Where there is hatred, let us sow love;
Where there is injury, pardon;
Where there is discord, union;
Where there is doubt, faith;
Where there is despair, hope;
Where there is darkness, light;
Where there is sadness, joy;
O Divine Master, Grant that we may not so much seek
To be consoled as to console,

To be understood as to understand,
To be loved as to love.
For it is in giving that we receive;
It is in pardoning that we are pardoned;
And it is in dying that we are born to eternal life.
Amen.

The Bride Adores Her Beloved, *Song of Solomon* 2:8–14 (ESV)

The voice of my beloved!
Behold, he comes,
leaping over the mountains,
bounding over the hills.
My beloved is like a gazelle
or a young stag.
Behold, there he stands
behind our wall,
gazing through the windows,
looking through the lattice.
My beloved speaks and says to me:
'Arise, my love, my beautiful one,
and come away,
for behold, the winter is past;
the rain is over and gone.
The flowers appear on the earth,
the time of singing has come,
and the voice of the turtledove
is heard in our land.
The fig tree ripens its figs,
and the vines are in blossom;
they give forth fragrance.
Arise, my love, my beautiful one,
and come away.
O my dove, in the clefts of the rock,
in the crannies of the cliff,
let me see your face,
let me hear your voice,
for your voice is sweet,
and your face is lovely.

Ruth 1:16–17

Do not press me to leave you, or turn back from following you!
Where you go, I will go;
Where you lodge, I will lodge;
your people will be my people,
and your God my God.
Where you die, I will die—
there to be buried.
May the Lord do thus and thus and so to me,
and more as well,
if even death parts me from you!

Colossians 3:12–14

Put on then, as God's chosen ones, holy and beloved, compassion, kindness, lowliness, meekness, and patience, forbearing one another and, if one has a complaint against another, forgiving each other; as the Lord has forgiven you, so you also must forgive. And above all these put on love, which binds everything together in perfect harmony.

Ecclesiastes 4:9–12

Two are better than one, because they have a good return for their toil. For if they fall, one will lift up his fellow; but woe to him who is alone when he falls and has not another to lift him up. Again, if two lie together, they are warm; but how can one be warm alone? And though a man might prevail against one who is alone, two will withstand him.

CHAPTER ELEVEN
CONTACTS

Wedding websites

There are so many wedding websites out there—it's frightening! However, they can provide you with lots of ideas and wisdom. The chat rooms can be particularly useful when looking for locations for weddings and so on. Most of them have contact details for civil celebrants as well.

Australia and New Zealand

www.i-do.com.au—One of the most popular wedding sites in Australia but mainly concentrating on the east coast.

www.weddings.co.nz—New Zealand's premier online wedding magazine and directory.

www.yourwedding.com.au—Website of *Your Wedding* magazine, concentrating mainly on New South Wales.

www.newlywed.com.au—Includes kits for changing your name,

quill pens for signing the registry and pillows for ring ceremonies.

The following group of sites has excellent chat rooms which you can browse and find out interesting places that others have married in and so on:

www.weddingwa.com.au
www.weddingsa.com.au
www.weddingvic.com.au
wvvw.weddingnsw.com.au

International

www.weddingguide.co.uk—Lots of ideas and even MP3 samples of music that you can listen to. ·

www.confetti.co.uk/weddings/—Big UK site with loads of information and ideas on cross-cultural weddings and song ideas.

www.take2weddings.com—Part of the Confetti network, this site focuses on people making the walk the second time around. It has lots of great ideas for themes and practical advice on issues such as how to include children.

www.theknot.com—Another huge American site. Scary in the depths that it trawls but lots of useful tips and advice.

www.just-wedding-favors.com—A great web site for ideas if you are interested in themes: Irish, autumn, midsummer night's dream, or environmental.

Bridal magazines

Some bridal magazines, from the United States in particular, have excellent websites with lots of information that can be helpful when planning your marriage ceremony.

www.modernbride.com—*Modern Bride*
www.brides.com—*Brides*
www.usabride.com—*USA Bride*

www.marthastewart.com—Martha Stewart has fallen out of favour in recent times but the wedding section has some useful tips and pictures on Jewish and Christian weddings.

Celebrants

www.celebrantsonline.com.au—Celebrants Online. An excellent source of contacts in Victoria as well as other states.

www.civilcelebrants.com.au—The Australian Federation of Civil Celebrants.

www.celebranz.org.nz.—Celebrants Association of New Zealand.

www.celebrant.co.nz—New Zealand Celebrant Directory.

www.monashcelebrants.net.au/index.html—List of graduates of the first post graduate, public university-run civil celebrancy course in Australia.

www.ag.gov.au—Commonwealth Attorney General's website. If you type in 'marriage celebrants program' at this address you will find information about the program plus a list of every marriage celebrant authorised by the department.

Civil marriage celebrants

Geoffrey Baird
Melbourne, Australia
Mobile: 0412 073 081
Website: www.geoffreybaird.com/civcel/civcel-index.html

Catherine Bearsley
Melbourne, Australia
Mobile: (0412) 066 722
Email: cbearsley@optusnet.com.au

Jocelyn Fausett
Civil Marriage Celebrant and Life Coach
Auckland, New Zealand
Tel: (09) 309 8117
Email: jj.fausett@xtra.co.nz
Website: www.jjfausett.co.nz

Norman Knipe
Upper Hutt, Wellington, New Zealand
Tel: (04) 528 5888
Email: norman.knipe@paradise.net.nz
Website: www.celebrant.dns2go.com

Pat Lane
Melbourne, Australia
Tel: (03) 5762 1707; Mobile: (0439) 721 707
Email: pat.lane@bigpond.com

Nitza Lowenstein
Sydney, Australia
Mobile: 0418 453 865
Email: lowens@bigpond.net.au

June Newman
Gosford, NSW, Australia
Mobile: (0407) 341 148
Website: www.junenewman.com

Myly Nguyen
Melbourne, Australia
Tel: (03) 9327 2969; Mobile: (0438) 252 260
Email: mylyn@alphalink.com.au

Judy Peiris
Melbourne, Australia
Tel: (03) 9874 1965; Mobile: (0417) 322 173
Email: civiljude@hotmail.con

Clive Rumney
Melbourne, Australia
Tel: (03) 9852 8410
Email: crumney@netspace.net.au

Judy Seregin
Tel: (03) 9728 6810; Mobile: (0409) 960 070
Email: judys@hilink.com.au

Cherie Scott
Spiritual and Civil Celebrant
Warranwood, Victoria, Australia
Tel: (03) 9876 5005
Email: scojoc@ozemail.com.au

Marita Wilcox
Melbourne, Australia
Tel: (03) 9416 1096; Mobile: (0419) 398 910
Queensland, Australia
Tel: (07) 5526 5675; Mobile: (0419) 398 910
Email: maritawilcox@bigpond.com

Pre-marriage education providers and counsellors

Relationships Australia
National Office
15 Napier Close,
Deakin ACT 2600
Australia
(PO Box 320, Curtin ACT 2605, Australia)
Tel: (02) 6281 3600 (All general and counselling enquiries/
appointments)
Freecall: 1300 364 277
Website: www.relationships.com.au

Relationship Services Whakawhanaungatanga
This organisation is a leading provider of counselling and education
services in New Zealand.
Tel: 0800 735 283
Email: receptn@relate.org.nz
Website: www.relate.org.nz

Marriage and Relationship Educators' Association of Australia (MAREAA)
PO Box 277, Mitcham S.C.,
SA 5062
Australia
Tel / Fax: (08) 6210 1746
Website: www.meaa.asn.au

www.relate.gov.au—For information on relationships, family, love and life.

www.csme.catholic.org.au—Catholic Society for Marriage Education.

www.smartmarriages.com—A leading US site on making marriage work.

www.stepfamily.asn.au—Stepfamily Association of South Australia Inc. A useful site offering advice on how to make step families work.

Religion

www.about.com/religion—A good starting point for all the basics on the world's religions.

www.cofe.anglican.org/commonworship/marriage/marriage.html—The UK division of the Church of England, jam-packed with loads of ideas for Anglican marriage services.

www.vatican.va—The website of the Vatican—If you search for marriage service and trawl through piles of documents, you will find all sorts of material that you may be able to use.

www.goarch.org—Another comprehensive website for the Greek Orthodox church in the United States—loads of information.

Butterfly releasing companies

Butterfly Magic
New Zealand
Tel: (07) 8532 068
Email: info@butterflymagic.co.nz
Website: www.butterflymagic.co.nz

Butterfly Impressions
South Australia
Tel: (08) 9840 9257
Website: www.butterfly-impressions.com/

Butterfly Brilliance
Australia
Tel: 1300 300 800
Website: www.butterflybrilliance.com.au

Readings

Most of the large wedding websites have a good selection of poetry. If you do a general search on the Internet and type in the words 'love poems', you will be inundated with choices. Listed below are some other places you might find something that resonates with you.

www.poets.org—Sponsored by The Academy of American Poets, this site offers find 1400 poems from the famous to the yet-to-be discovered.

www.poetry.com—Claims to be 'the largest and most comprehensive poetry site on the net'. See what you think.

www.allspirit.co.uk/poetryindex.html—If you are looking for something beyond the usual suspects, this site may interest you. It features works by Omar Khayyam and Maya Angelou.

www.bible.gospelcom.net—This is a great Bible website. You can choose which version of the Bible you would like to draw from.

www.eir.library.utoronto.ca/rpo/display_rpo/intro.cfm—Representative Poetry Online. On this site you'll find works by over 400 poets.

Registries of Births, Deaths and Marriages in Australia

Victoria

Registry of Births, Deaths and Marriages
GPO Box 4332
Melbourne VIC 3001
Tel: 1300 369 367; Fax: (03) 9603 5880

New South Wales

Registry of Births, Deaths and Marriages
GPO Box 30
Sydney NSW 2001
Tel: 1300 655 236; Fax: (02) 9699 8906

Queensland

Registry of Births, Deaths and Marriages
GPO Box 188
Albert Street
Brisbane QLD 4000
Tel: (07) 3247 9203; Fax: (07) 3247 5803

Western Australia

Registry of Births, Deaths and Marriages
PO Box 7720
Cloisters Square
Perth WA 6850
Tel: (08) 9264 1555; Fax: (08) 9264 1599

Tasmania

Registry of Births, Deaths and Marriages
GPO Box 198
Hobart TAS 7001
Tel: (03) 6233 3793; Fax: (03) 6233 6444

Northern Territory

Registry of Births, Deaths and Marriages
GPO Box 3021
Darwin NT 8001
Tel: (08) 8999 6119; Fax: (08) 8999 6324

Alice Springs

Registry of Births, Deaths and Marriages
GPO Box 8043
Alice Springs NT 0871
Tel: (08) 8951 5339

Australian Capital Territory

Registry of Births, Deaths and Marriages
GPO Box 788
Canberra ACT 2601
Tel: (02) 6207 0460

Registries of Births, Deaths and Marriages in New Zealand

Auckland

Registrar of Births, Deaths and Marriages
Level 6
AA Building
99 Albert Street
Auckland
Tel: 0800 22 52 52; Fax: (09) 362 7908

Christchurch

Registrar of Births, Deaths and Marriages
Private Bag 25-211
48 Peterborough Street
Christchurch
Tel: (03) 379 6006; Fax: (03) 366 9141

Manukau

Registrar of Births, Deaths and Marriages
Corner Amersham Way and Osterley Way
PO Box 76-222
Manukau City
Tel: (09) 263 6522; Fax: (09) 262 2404

Wellington

Registrar of Births, Deaths and Marriages
Level 3, Boulcott House
47 Boulcott Street
Wellington
(PO Box 10-526, Wellington)
Tel: (04) 474 8150; Fax: (04) 474 8147

REFERENCES

The Archbishops' Council 2000, *Book of Common Worship*, Church of England, http://www.cofe.anglican.org, 30/04/2004

'Blessing of the Hands' 2004, http://www.handfasting.com, 7/7/04

Bose, S. 2004, 'The Hindu Wedding Celebration', *Modern Bride*, http://www.modernbride.com, 7/7/04

Brownstein, R.M. 2002, *Jewish Weddings: A Beautiful Guide to Creating the Wedding of Your Dreams*, Simon & Schuster, New York

Champlin, Joseph M. 2002, *Together for Life*, Ave Maria Press, Notre Dame

Commonwealth of Australia 1961, *Marriage Act 1961*, Section 46(1)

—2001, *Happily Ever . . . Before and After*, Form 14A, *Marriage Act 1961*

—2002, *Two Equals One*, Department of Family and Community Services, Canberra

—2004, Marriages and Divorces, Australia, ABS Catalogue No. 3310.0

'Cost of love survey results' 2004, *Bride to Be* http://www.ido.com.au, 30/04/2004

Darby, Andrew 2004, 'Tasmania accepts same-sex partners', *The Age*, 3 January

Ferguson, Joy 2001, 'Pagan Handfasting Traditions for Your Sacred Union', *Magickal Wedding*, ECW Press, Toronto

Fitzgerald, T. 2004, The Sacraments, *Greek Orthodox Archdiocese of America*, http://www.goarch.org 7/7/04

Gross, Samantha 1999, 'The Secrets of a Blooming Cosmetics Success With Glimmer Gloss and Eyebrow Fetishes, an Australian Offers an Irreverent Alternative', *Forward*, http://www.forward.com, 7/7/04

Hawkhurst, Joan C. 1997, *Interfaith Wedding Ceremonies: Samples and Sources*, Dovetail Publishing, Boston

Javes, Sue 2004, 'Margaret Throsby understands the key to a good confession,. The Guide, *Sydney Morning Herald*, 29 March, Late edition, p. 3

Juster-Schofield, T. 2001, *Medieval Wedding Ceremony*, Melbourne

Kaldera, R. and Schwartzstein, T. 2004, *Handfasting and Wedding Rituals*, Llewellyn Publications, St Paul

Kingma, D.R. 1991, *Weddings from the Heart*, Conari Press, Emeryville

Lerner, D.A. 1999, *Celebrating Interfaith Marriages*, Henry Holt, New York

Llywelyn, Morgan 2002, *Finn Mac Cool*, Tor Books, New York

Metrick, S.B. 1992, *I Do*, First Celestial Arts Printing, California

Miller, Henry 1987, *Sexus*, Grove Press, New York

Ministry of Justice New Zealand 1999, *Same-Sex Couples and the Law—Backgrounding the Issues*

Music for the Royal Wedding in Copenhagen Cathedral 2004, *Prince of Denmark's website*, http://www.hkhkronprinsen.dk, 7/7/2004

Nance, Deborah 2003, *e bulletin for marriage celebrants*, November

Newman, M. 2004, *Stepfamily Life: Why it is different—And How to Make it Work*, Finch Publishing, Sydney

New Zealand Department of Internal Affairs 2004, Registrar of Births, Deaths and Marriages, *How to get a marriage licence?* http://wwwv.bdm.govt.nz/diawebsite.nsf/wpg_URL/Services-Births-Deaths-and-Marriages-How-to-Get-a-Marriage-Licence? OpenDocument, 5/7/2004

New Zealand Electronic Poetry Centre http://www.nzepc.auckland.ac.nz, 30/04/04

New Zealand Law Society 2002, *Dividing up Relationship Property*

—2003, *Making a Will and Estate Administration*

Nolo 2004, *Marriage Requirements, Procedures and Ceremonies*, http://www.nolo.com, 5/7/2004

Tresidder, J. 1997, *The Hutchinson Dictionary of Symbols*, Duncan Baird Publishing, London

Tunnah, Helen 2004, 'More MPs support relationships bill', *The New Zealand Herald*, 30 June

'We were never married, says Jagger' 2004, *The Irish Examiner*, http://archives.tcm.ie/irishexaminer/1999/0l/19/fhead.htm, 23/4/2004

Wood, Charlotte 2002, 'Do you, Jane, take this man's name?' *Sydney Morning Herald*, 27 July, Late edition, Spectrum, p. 8

Poetry References

Auden, W.H. 'O Tell Me the Truth About Love', http://www.weddingguide.co.uk, 10/10/04

——2004, 'How Do I Love Thee', http://www.poets.org, 10/10/04

Baynes, C.F. 1997, *The I Ching or Book of Changes*, Princeton University Press, Princeton

Brown, Timothy 2004, *Psalms and Compassions: A Jesuit's Journey Through Cancer*, Resonant Publishing, Baltimore

Browning, Elizabeth Barrett, 1986, *Sonnets from the Portuguese: A Celebration of Love*, St Martin's Press, New York

Byron, George Gordon 1990, *The Love Poems of Lord Byron: A Romantic's Passion*, St Martin's Press, New York

Clark, John Cooper 1982, 'I Wanna Be Yours', http://www.cyberspike.com, 10/10/04

De Bernieres, Louis 1994, *Captain Corelli's Mandolin*, Vintage, New York

De Saint-Exupery, Antoine, *The Little Prince*, http://www.spiritual.com.au, 12/10/04

Dickinson, Emily 1961, *The Complete Poems of Emily Dickinson*, Little Brown, New York

Donno, Elizabeth Story (ed) 1996, *Andrew Marvell The Complete Poems*, Penguin Books, London

Duffy, Carol Ann 2004, Warming Her Pearls, For Judith Radstone, http://www.geocities.com, 10/10/04

Duhan, Johnny, 'The Voyage', http://www.johnnyduhan.com, 12/10/04

Eluard, Paul 1951, *La Pléiade*, T2 P403, Gallimard, Paris

Forster, E.M. *A Room With a View*, http://www.online-literature.com, 10/10/04

Frost, Robert 1969, *The Poetry of Robert Frost*, Henry Holt, New York

Gibran, Kahlil 2001, *The Prophet*, Knopf, New York

Griffin, Susan 2004, Love Should Grow Up Like a Wild Iris in the Fields, http://www.panhala.net, 10/10/2004

Harmon, William 1992, *The Top 500 Poems*, Columbia University Press, New York

Hughes, Ted 2003, *Collected Poems*, Farrar, Straus and Giroux, New York

Jones, Alexander 1968, *The Jerusalem Bible*, Doubleday, New York

Lawrence, D.H 2004, 'Fidelity', http://www.eharlequin.com, 10/10/2004

Lennon John, 1984, 'Grow Old With Me', http://www.lyricsdepot.com, 10/10/04

Linfield, Jordan and Krevisky, Joseph 1993, *Words of Love: Romantic Quotations from Plato to Madonna*, Gramercy Books, New York

Marlowe, Christopher 2004, 'The Passionate Shepherd to His Love', http://www.bartleby.com, 10/10/04

McCulloch, Patty 1999, *Take Ten for Prayer*, Ave Maria Press, Notre Dame

Milne, AA 1988, *Now We Are Six*, Penguin Books, New York

Morrison, Toni 1987, *Beloved*, Penguin Books, New York

Mountain Dreamer, Oriah 1999, *The Invitation*, HarperCollins, New York

Nash, Ogden, 'Reprise', http://www.geocities.com, 12/10/04

Patton, Beth Ann 2004, *Laughter Is The Spice Of Life*, Publishing Group, Nashville

Pockell, Leslie 2003, *The 100 Best Love Poems of All Time*, Warner Books, New York

Powell, Anne 'Aotearoa Litany', http://www.lifecelebrations.co.nz, 12/10/04

Rilke, Rainer, 'Maria On Marriage', http://www.verticalpool.com, 12/10/04

Roney, Carla 2000, *The Knot Guide to Wedding Vows and Traditions: Readings, Rituals, Music, Dances, and Toasts*, Broadway Books, New York

Rossetti, Christina 2004, 'The First Day', http://www.greatlovepoems.com, 10/10/04

Shakespeare, William 1957, Sonnet XVII in *Love Poems & Sonnets of William Shakespeare*, Doubleday, New York, p.11

—1993, *Twelfth Night*, Washington Square Press, New York

St Francis of Assisi, 'The Prayer', http://www.aahistory.com, 12/10/04

Yeats, William Butler 2004, 'He Wishes for the Cloths of Heaven', http://www.poetryconnection.net, 10/10/04

—2004, 'When You are Old', http://www.bartleby.com, 10/10/04

Whitman, Walt 1982, *Walt Whitman: Poetry and Prose*, Literary Classics of the United States, Library of America, New York

BIBLIOGRAPHY

Aridas, C. 2003, *Your Catholic Wedding*, Crossroad Publishing Company, New York

Best, A. & Hunt, J. 1997, *Weddings*, Hodder & Stoughton, London,

Champlin, Joseph M. 2003, *Together for Life*, Ave Maria Press, Notre Dame

Chevalier, J. & Gheerbrant A. 1996, *Dictionary of Symbols*, Penguin, London

Ferguson, Joy 2001, *Magickal Weddings*, ECW Press, Toronto

Howard, Rod 2000, *Getting Hitched*, Hardie Grant Books, South Yarra

Hudson, H. 2001, *Vows*, Priory Press, Otaki

Kaldera, R. & Schwartzstein, T. 2004, *Handfasting and Wedding Rituals*, Llewellyn Publications, St Paul

Kingma, Daphne Rose 1991, *Weddings from the Heart*, Conari Press, California

Levin, L. & Bellotti, G. 1994, *Creative Weddings*, Plume, New York

Messenger, Dally R. 1999, *Ceremonies and Celebrations*, Lothian Books, Melbourne

Metrick, S.B. 1992, *I Do—A Guide To Creating Your Own Unique Wedding Ceremony*, Celestial Arts, Berkeley

Reekie, J. 1992, *Ritz Book of Weddings*, William Morrow and Company, New York

Ross-Macdonald, J. 1996, *Alternative Weddings*, Thomson, San Francisco

Tresidder, J. 1997, *The Hutchinson Dictionary of Symbols*, Duncan Baird Publishing, London

Wiener, Nancy H. 2001, *Beyond Breaking the Glass*, CCAR Press, New York

CREDITS

The authors and publishers are grateful to many individuals and organisations who gave us permission to use their work. These include:

Songs

'Grow old with me' by John Lennon © 1984 Lenono Music/ EMI Music Publishing Australia Pty Ltd.

'Somebody' by Martin Gore © 1984 Grabbing Hands Music Ltd/ EMI Music Publishing Australia Pty Ltd.

'I Wanna Be Yours' by J.C Clarke, M. Hannett, S. Hopkins © 1982 EMI Songs Ltd/ EMI Music Publishing Australia Pty Ltd.

'You're The Best Thing' (Weller) © Stylist Music Ltd/BMG Music Publishing Ltd. Used with kind permission by BMG Music Publishing Australia Pty Ltd. All rights reserved.

Book extracts

Poems

'Aoetora Litany' by Anne Powell. Reprinted with permission from Anne Powell.

Television

Wedding vows of Thorne and Macy, from the 'Bold and the Beautiful', reproduced with permission from David Gregg, International Publicity, The Bold and the Beautiful, CBS Television City, Los Angeles.

INDEX